HOUGHTON MIFFLIN HARCOURT

TEXAS JOURNEYS

Program Authors

James F. Baumann · David J. Chard · Jamal Cooks
J. David Cooper · Russell Gersten · Marjorie Lipson
Lesley Mandel Morrow · John J. Pikulski · Héctor H. Rivera
Mabel Rivera · Shane Templeton · Sheila W. Valencia
Catherine Valentino · MaryEllen Vogt

Consulting Author
Irene Fountas

HOUGHTON MIFFLIN HARCOURT
School Publishers

HOUGHTON MIFFLIN HARCOURT

Texas
JOURNEYS

HOUGHTON MIFFLIN HARCOURT
School Publishers

Unit 4

EXTREME NATURE

Big Idea Our world is an amazing place!

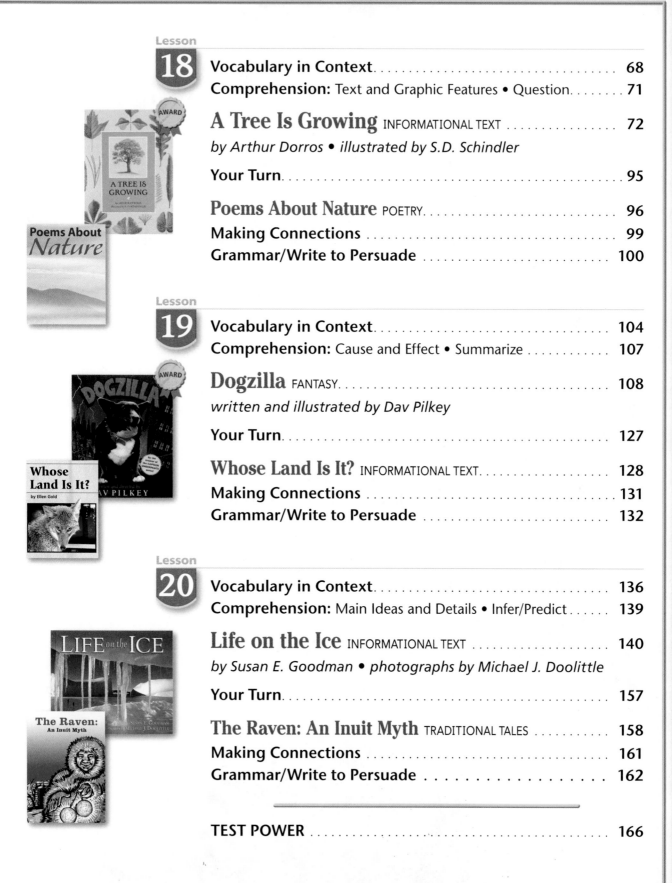

Unit 5

Going Places

💡 **Big Idea** There are many reasons to take a journey.

EXTREME
NATURE

unit 4

Big Idea

Our world is an
amazing place!

Paired Selections

recycle

project

dripping

carton

complicated

pollution

rubbish

hardly

shade

global

Vocabulary Reader   Context Cards

TEKS 3.4B use context to determine word meaning; **ELPS 3D** speak using content-area vocabulary

Vocabulary in Context

1   recycle

When people recycle old bottles, the glass can be used again.

2   project

This garden is a neighborhood project. Many people work on it.

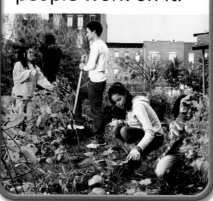

3   dripping

This faucet is dripping water. Each drop of water is wasted.

4   carton

A carton, or light cardboard container, can be recycled after use.

- **Study each Context Card.**

- **Make up a new context sentence that uses two Vocabulary words.**

5 complicated

One complicated, or difficult, part of recycling can be sorting plastic.

6 pollution

Noise pollution, or too many loud sounds, can be bad for our hearing.

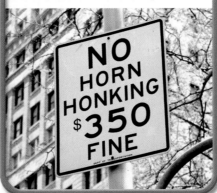

7 rubbish

The more rubbish, or trash, people make, the more room it takes up.

8 hardly

Some light bulbs use a lot of energy. This bulb uses hardly any energy.

9 shade

The shade from this tree keeps the house cool in the summer.

10 global

Air pollution is a global problem. It affects people all over the world.

Background

✓ TARGET VOCABULARY **Don't Dump It** Some towns burn rubbish, but burning waste causes air pollution. Other towns bury trash, but there is hardly any room left in landfills. Too much trash is a global problem. The solution is not complicated. People need to recycle! Make recycling a family project. Rinse and sort those dripping bottles and cans into bins. Flatten that carton and tie it up with newspapers. Recycle kitchen scraps by making compost. It will become fertilizer for your garden.

How to Compost

1 Green yard waste, fruit and vegetable scraps, coffee grounds, tea leaves

2 Dry leaves, straw, sawdust, wood chips, dried grass, shredded cardboard or newspaper

3 Moist soil, ash, fertilizer

Compost in the sun, not the shade. Add water and mix the pile every now and then to give it air.

Comprehension

✔ TARGET SKILL **Author's Purpose**

Story details give clues about why the author wrote "A Mr. Rubbish Mood." They also give clues to help you figure out the author's theme, or message. Use a chart like this to list details that give clues about the theme. Use the clues to write in your own words what the theme is.

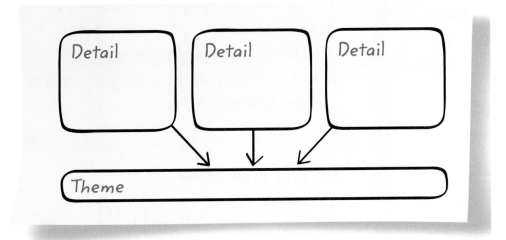

✔ TARGET STRATEGY **Monitor/Clarify**

As you read, monitor and clarify any story details that are unclear. Understanding these details can help you figure out the author's purpose and the theme.

✓ **TARGET VOCABULARY**

recycle	pollution
project	rubbish
dripping	hardly
carton	shade
complicated	global

✓ **TARGET SKILL**

Author's Purpose Use text details to tell why an author writes a book.

✓ **TARGET STRATEGY**

Monitor/Clarify As you read, find a way to clear up what doesn't make sense.

GENRE
Humorous fiction is a story written to entertain readers. Who is the narrator in this story, the author or a story character? How would the story change if it were told from a different point of view?

 TEKS 3.8C identify narrator as first/third person; **ELPS 4K** employ analytical skills to demonstrate comprehension

MEET THE AUTHOR
Megan McDonald

Once while Megan McDonald was visiting a school, some students asked her, "Are you ever in a bad mood?" This got her thinking about creating a character with lots of different moods. Judy Moody was born! Many of Judy Moody's adventures actually happened to McDonald when she was a child.

MEET THE ILLUSTRATOR
Peter H. Reynolds

Peter Reynolds and his twin brother started writing their own books when they were about seven. Reynolds has been drawing and telling stories ever since. After illustrating more than seven Judy Moody books, he feels like Judy Moody's family is part of his own family.

A Mr. Rubbish Mood

from Judy Moody Saves the World!

by Megan McDonald

illustrated by Peter H. Reynolds

Essential Question

Why do some authors write funny stories?

It was still dark out when Judy woke up early the next morning. She found her flashlight and notebook. Then she tiptoed downstairs to the kitchen and started to save the world.

She hoped she could save the world before breakfast. Judy wondered if other people making the world a better place had to do it quietly, and in the dark, so their parents would not wake up.

She, Judy Moody, was in a Mr. Rubbish mood. Mr. Rubbish was the Good Garbage Gremlin in her brother Stink's comic book, who built his house out of French-fry cartons and pop bottles. He recycled everything, even lollipop sticks. And he never used anything from the rain forest.

Hmmm . . . things that came from the rain forest. That would be a good place to start. Rubber came from the rain forest. And chocolate and spices and things like perfume. Even chewing gum.

Judy collected stuff from around the house and piled it on the kitchen table. Chocolate bars, brownie mix, vanilla ice cream. Her dad's coffee beans. The rubber toilet plunger. Gum from Stink's gumball machine. Her mom's lipstick from the bottom of her purse. She was so busy saving the rain forest that she didn't hear her family come into the kitchen.

"What in the world . . . ?" Mom said.

"Judy, why are you in the dark?" Dad asked, turning on the lights.

"Hey, my gumball machine!" Stink said.

Judy held out her arms to block the way. "We're not going to use this stuff anymore. It's all from the rain forest," she told them.

"Says who?" asked Stink.

"Says Mr. Rubbish. They cut down way too many trees to grow coffee and give us makeup and chewing gum. The earth is our home. We have to take action to save it. We don't need all this stuff."

"I need gum!" yelled Stink. "Give me back my gum!"

"Stink! Don't yell. Haven't you ever heard of noise pollution?"

"Is my coffee in there?" Dad asked, rubbing his hair.

"Judy? Is that ice cream? It's dripping all over the table!" Mom carried the leaky carton over to the sink.

"ZZZZ-ZZZZZ!" Judy made the sound of a chain saw cutting down trees.

"She's batty," Stink said.

Dad put the brownie mix back in the cupboard. Mom took the toilet plunger off the kitchen table and headed for the bathroom.

Time for Plan B. Project R.E.C.Y.C.L.E. She, Judy Moody, would show her family just how much they hurt the planet. Every time someone threw something away, she would write it down. She got her notebook and looked in the trash can. She wrote down:

1 orange juice can
1 inside of peanut butter jar lid
1 plastic bread bag
4 broken eggshells
smelly yucky wet coffee grounds
3 paper muffin holders
2 smooshed Scarlett O'cherry Juice Boxes (and straws!)
½ Bowl of oatmeal

"Stink! You shouldn't throw gooey old oatmeal in the trash!" Judy said.

"Dad! Tell her to quit spying on me."

"I'm a Garbage Detective!" said Judy. "*Garbologist* to you. If you want to learn what to recycle, you have to get to know your garbage."

"Here," said Stink, sticking something wet and mushy under Judy's nose. "Get to know my apple core."

"Hardee-har-har," said Judy. "Hasn't anybody in this family ever heard of the Three R's?"

"The Three R's?" asked Dad.

"Re-use. Re-cycle."

"What's the third one?" asked Stink.

"Re-fuse to talk to little brothers until they quit throwing stuff away."

"Mom! I'm not going to stop throwing stuff away just because Judy's having a trash attack."

"Look at all this stuff we throw away!" Judy said. "Did you know that one person throws away more than eight pounds of garbage a day?"

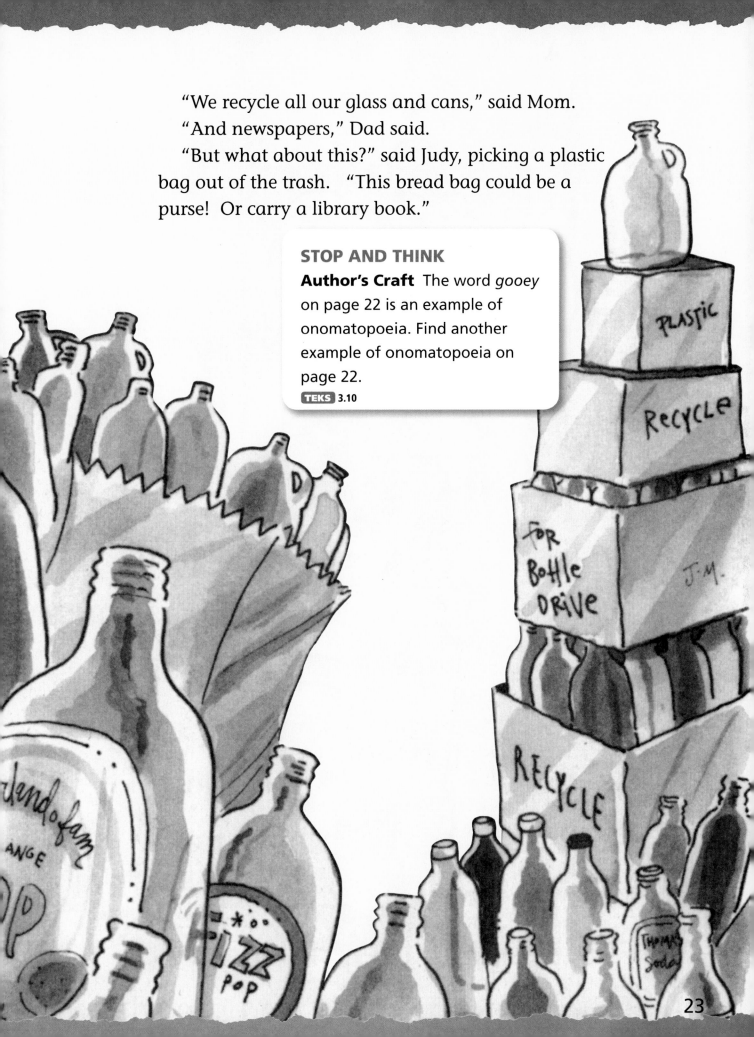

"We recycle all our glass and cans," said Mom.

"And newspapers," Dad said.

"But what about this?" said Judy, picking a plastic bag out of the trash. "This bread bag could be a purse! Or carry a library book."

STOP AND THINK

Author's Craft The word *gooey* on page 22 is an example of onomatopoeia. Find another example of onomatopoeia on page 22.

TEKS 3.10

24

"What's so great about eggshells?" asked Stink. "And smelly old ground-up coffee?"

"You can use them to feed plants. Or make compost." Just then, something in the trash caught her eye. A pile of wooden craft sticks? Judy pulled it out. "Hey! My Laura Ingalls Wilder log cabin I made in second grade!"

"It looks like a glue museum to me," said Stink.

"I'm sorry, Judy," Mom said. "I should have asked first, but we can't save everything, honey."

"Recycle it!" said Stink. "You could use it for kindling, to start a fire! Or break it down in toothpicks."

"Not funny, Stink."

"Judy, you're not even ready for school yet. Let's talk about this later," said Dad. "It's time to get dressed."

It was no use. Nobody listened to her. Judy trudged upstairs, feeling like a sloth without a tree.

"I won't wear lipstick today if it'll make you feel better," Mom called up the stairs.

"And I'll only drink half a cup of coffee," Dad said, but Judy could hardly hear him over the grinding of the rain forest coffee beans.

✔ STOP AND THINK

Monitor/Clarify Does Stink believe Judy should use her log cabin for kindling or toothpicks, or is there another reason he said this?

TEKS 3.8B

Her family sure knew how to ruin a perfectly good Mr. Rubbish mood. She put on her jeans and her Spotted Owl T-shirt. And to save water, she did not brush her teeth.

She clomped downstairs in a mad-at-your-whole-family mood.

"Here's your lunch," said Mom.

"Mom! It's in a paper bag!"

"What's wrong with that?" Stink asked.

"Don't you get it?" said Judy. "They cut down trees to make paper bags. Trees give shade. They help control global warming. We would die without trees. They make oxygen and help take dust and stuff out of the air."

"Dust!" said Mom. "Let's talk about cleaning your room if we're going to talk about dust."

"Mo-om!" How was she supposed to do important things like save trees if she couldn't even save her *family* tree? That did it. Judy went straight to the garage and dug out her Sleeping Beauty lunch box from kindergarten.

STOP AND THINK

Author's Purpose Who is more convincing in the story, Judy or her family? What might this tell you about the author's opinion of recycling?

"Are you really going to take that baby lunch box on the bus? Where the whole world can see?" asked Stink.

"I'm riding my bike today," said Judy. "To save energy."

"See you at school, then." Stink waved his *paper-bag* lunch at her. If only she could recycle her little brother.

"Go ahead. Be a tree hater," called Judy.

Making the world a better place sure was complicated.

Your Turn

1. What is the main reason that Judy Moody is angry at the end of the story?

   ⬭ She did not sleep well the night before.

   ⬭ Her family did not take her seriously.

   ⬭ Her dad made coffee.

   ⬭ She has to ride a bike to school.

   TEKS 3.8B

2. ✔ TARGET SKILL **Author's Purpose**

   In A Mr. Rubbish Mood, the author wants to inform readers about recycling. She also wants to make them laugh. On a chart like this, list the parts of the story that show how the author entertains readers. **TEKS** 3.2B

3. ✔ TARGET STRATEGY **Monitor/Clarify**

   The author uses slang, or casual speech, to add humor to the story. Find some examples of slang. Tell what each word or phrase means. **TEKS** 3.4D **ELPS** 1F

4. **Oral Language** Use the Retelling Cards to tell a partner how Judy tried to save the world. Then explain which part of the story you liked best, and why. **ELPS** 4G

   Retelling Cards

 TEKS TEKS **3.2B** ask questions/clarify/locate facts/details/use text evidence; **3.4D** identify/apply playful language uses; **3.8B** describe characters' relationships/changes; **ELPS 1F** use accessible language to learn new language; **4G** demonstrate comprehension through shared reading/retelling/responding/note-taking

29

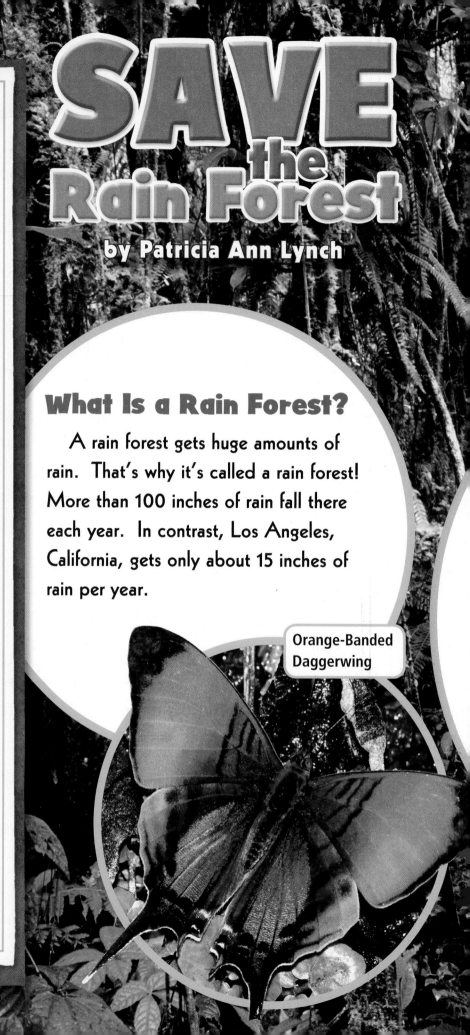

SAVE the Rain Forest

by Patricia Ann Lynch

What Is a Rain Forest?

A rain forest gets huge amounts of rain. That's why it's called a rain forest! More than 100 inches of rain fall there each year. In contrast, Los Angeles, California, gets only about 15 inches of rain per year.

Orange-Banded Daggerwing

Monteverde Rain Forest, Costa Rica

Toco Toucan

Rain Forest Plants

A rain forest has hundreds of kinds of trees and flowers. Under your feet is a carpet of leaves. Moisture is dripping everywhere. Hardly any light reaches the ground because tall trees form a canopy, or upper layer, high above. It hides the sky and provides shade.

Rain Forest Animals

A rain forest is noisy! Birds squawk. Thousands of insects buzz and hum. Monkeys chatter in the trees. Beetles grow as big as your hand. Some frogs grow as big as a milk carton!

Red-Eyed Leaf Frog

Why Are Rain Forests in Trouble?

Rain forests are important to life on Earth. They recycle. Tree roots use dead plants as food. Rain turns into clouds that make more rain. Trees take in carbon dioxide and give off the air we breathe.

Yet rain forests are in trouble. People cut down trees to get wood and land to farm. Most trees are not replaced. Many scientists think this may be a cause of global warming. Loggers also may leave rubbish behind. This is a kind of pollution.

The balance of life in a rain forest is complicated. Plants and animals depend on one another. If one dies out, others do, too.

Golden-Browed Chlorophonia

The Children's Rain Forest

In 1987, children in a Swedish school were studying rain forests. They learned that rain forests were in trouble. The class started a project to save a rain forest in Costa Rica. The class bought about 15 acres of land. This was the start of the Children's Rain Forest. This project works to save rain forests around the world.

Harvested logs in an Indonesian rain forest

Making Connections

TEKS 3.29A, 3.31; **ELPS** 2G, 3G

 Text to Self

Talk About Helping In *A Mr. Rubbish Mood*, Judy Moody reduces the use of rain forest products. Take turns in a group telling about something you do or would like to do to help the environment. Listen carefully to understand the main points of your classmates' topics. Ask questions to learn more.

TEKS 3.20B, RC-3(F); **ELPS** 5G

 Text to Text

Write a Letter In *A Mr. Rubbish Mood* and "Save the Rain Forest," you read about ways to save the rain forests. Write a letter to the editor of a newspaper that tells readers why the rain forests are in danger and three ways they can help.

TEKS 3.26A(iii)

 Text to World

Connect to Social Studies Research the locations of rain forests around the world. Show the class where the rain forests are by pointing to them on a map.

 TEKS **3.20B** write letters tailored to audience/purpose; **3.26A(iii)** collect information from visual sources; **3.29A** listen/ask questions/make comments; **3.31** participate in discussions/build on others' ideas; **RC-3(F)** make connections between texts; **ELPS** **2G** understand meaning/main points/details of spoken language; **3G** express opinions/ideas/feelings; **5G** narrate/describe/explain in writing

TEKS **3.22A(iii)** use/understand adjectives; **ELPS 5F** use a variety of sentence types in writing

Grammar

What Is an Adjective? An **adjective** is a word that describes, or tells about, a noun. Some adjectives tell what kind. Some tell how many.

Academic Language

adjective

Adjective
I recycle old cans.
A plastic bin holds the cans.
Nine cans are in the bin now.

Turn and Talk **Work with a partner. Read each sentence aloud. Identify the adjective in each sentence.**

❶ A loud noise awakened Tanya.

❷ Giant bottles were singing in Tanya's room!

❸ They were telling Tanya to recycle old bottles.

❹ Tanya tried many times to go back to sleep.

❺ Today she will recycle fifty bottles.

Sentence Fluency You can make your writing smooth and clear if you combine some sentences. If two short sentences tell about one noun, try combining the sentences by moving an adjective.

Connect Grammar to Writing

As you revise your persuasive letter, try moving adjectives to combine sentences.

Write to Persuade

✅ **Ideas** In *Judy Moody Saves the World*, Judy gives strong reasons for saving trees. When you revise your **persuasive letter**, think about the reasons you gave for your goal. Will they seem important to your reader?

Bianca wrote a letter persuading her neighbors to do more walking. Later, she changed some of her reasons to make them stronger.

Writing Traits Checklist

✅ **Ideas**
Did I state my goal and give strong reasons?

✅ **Organization**
Did I use correct letter form?

✅ **Word Choice**
Did I use polite language?

✅ **Voice**
Did I write in a positive tone?

✅ **Sentence Fluency**
Did I combine short, choppy sentences?

✅ **Conventions**
Did I use commas correctly? Did I write neatly in cursive?

Revised Draft

Dear Oak Hill Neighbors,

Let's take steps to become a healthier community. Walking steps!

~~If we walk more and drive less, we will all be better off.~~ Walking may take longer than driving, but ~~at least~~ it's great exercise that you can do all year round ~~you don't have to stop for traffic lights.~~

Another reason to walk is for cleaner air. Car fumes hurt our lungs and heart ~~That is an important reason.~~

36

182 Foster Street

Bentley, MO 23456

April 8, 2009

Oak Hill Neighborhood Organization

15 Cherry Street

Bentley, MO 23456

Dear Oak Hill Neighbors,

Let's take steps to become a healthier community. Walking steps! Walking may take longer than driving, but it's great exercise that you can do all year round. Another important reason to walk is for cleaner air. Car fumes hurt our lungs and heart. Finally, walking is relaxing because you can chat with neighbors and enjoy being outside. Let's all walk more for a healthier, happier community.

Sincerely,

Bianca Romano

> I gave strong reasons for my goal. I also combined two short sentences.

Reading as a Writer

Which sentence states Bianca's goal? Are the reasons important? Where can you give stronger reasons in your letter?

TARGET VOCABULARY

fossils

clues

remains

prove

evidence

skeletons

uncovering

buried

fierce

location

Vocabulary   Context
Reader   Cards

ELPS **3D** speak using content-area vocabulary; **4D** use prereading supports to comprehend texts

Vocabulary in Context

1 fossils
This man has found dinosaur fossils. He will learn a lot from the old bones.

2 clues
Fossils give clues that help scientists solve mysteries about dinosaurs.

3 remains
These are the remains of a large dinosaur. One bone is all that is left.

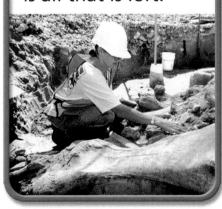

4 prove
Scientists are trying to prove, or show, that dinosaurs and birds are related.

- **Study each Context Card.**
- **Ask a question that uses one of the Vocabulary words.**

5 evidence

Egg fossils give evidence, or facts, about how dinosaurs raised their young.

6 skeletons

Scientists rarely find whole dinosaur skeletons like this one.

7 uncovering

Uncovering fossils takes time. The soil must be removed from around them.

8 buried

Many dinosaur bones buried, or covered, in mud turned into fossils.

9 fierce

Many people think of dinosaurs as fierce animals that fought all the time.

10 location

Sometimes many dinosaur bones are found in the same location.

Background

✓ **TARGET VOCABULARY** **Dig and Discover** Paleontologists are like science detectives. They use dinosaur fossils buried in the ground as clues to solve mysteries. Each new fossil provides evidence to help prove ideas, such as whether a dinosaur was fierce or gentle.

Sometimes paleontologists are lucky and find entire skeletons in a single location. Other times the remains of a creature may be only a few bones or teeth. Scientists can learn more about the past by uncovering fossils.

Carcharodontosaur

Why Did the Dinosaurs Disappear?

Idea 1	Idea 2	Idea 3
▼	▼	▼
A giant asteroid hit Earth.	The climate, or Earth's long-term weather, changed.	Huge volcanoes erupted.
▼	▼	▼
Dust and gas blocked sunlight.	Plants dinosaurs ate died.	Ash and gas from volcanoes blocked sunlight.
▼	▼	▼
Dinosaurs died of cold.	Dinosaurs died from hunger.	Dinosaurs died of cold.

Comprehension

✔ TARGET SKILL Conclusions

As you read *The Albertosaurus Mystery*, use text clues to draw conclusions, or make smart guesses, about what it's like to be a fossil hunter. Write text clues in a chart like this. Then use the text clues to help you draw a conclusion.

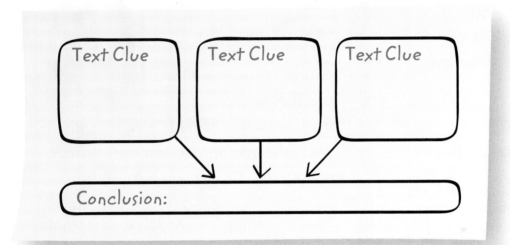

Text Clue   Text Clue   Text Clue

Conclusion:

✔ TARGET STRATEGY Visualize

Use details from *The Albertosaurus Mystery* to help you visualize, or picture, what the author describes. Then draw conclusions about what it's like to hunt fossils.

JOURNEYS DIGITAL **Powered by** DESTINATIONReading®
Comprehension Activities: Lesson 17

The ALBERTOSAURUS MYSTERY

✔ **TARGET VOCABULARY**

fossils	skeletons
clues	uncovering
remains	buried
prove	fierce
evidence	location

✔ **TARGET SKILL**

Conclusions Use text details to figure out ideas the author doesn't state.

✔ **TARGET STRATEGY**

Visualize As you read, use selection details to picture what is happening.

GENRE

Informational text gives factual information about a topic.

MEET THE AUTHOR

T. V. PADMA

T. V. Padma, whose full name is Dr. Padma Venkatraman, has a lot of different interests. She loves science, math, nature, animals, space, the ocean, fossils, music, history, and poetry. Padma was born in India. She lives in Rhode Island now, where she enjoys canoeing, hiking, and horseback riding.

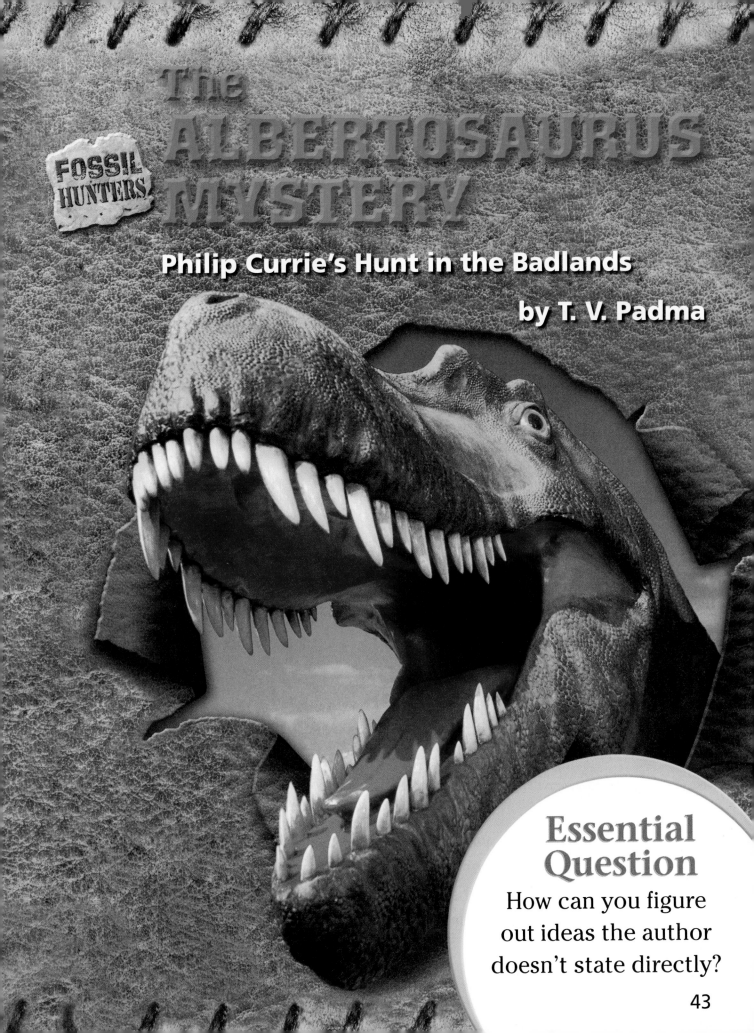

The ALBERTOSAURUS MYSTERY

FOSSIL HUNTERS

Philip Currie's Hunt in the Badlands

by T. V. Padma

Essential Question

How can you figure out ideas the author doesn't state directly?

Searching Without a Map

Many fossils are buried in Canada's badlands. More than 40 kinds of dinosaurs once lived there.

Philip Currie was thirsty and tired. It was one of the hottest summer days of 1997. He and his team were looking for fossils that belonged to a dinosaur called *Albertosaurus* (al bur toh SOHR uhs).

The badlands of western Canada are full of hills.
Philip didn't know which hill held Brown's fossils.

Almost 90 years earlier, a famous fossil hunter named Barnum Brown had found a fossil field in western Canada's badlands. Many albertosaurs were buried in it. Philip was trying to find this place again.

It was like looking for a needle in a haystack. Brown had not made a map or written down where he had found the fossils. Philip had few clues—just some notes and four old photos.

Discovery!

The team was running out of water. Everyone except Philip went back to the camp. He continued on with the search. Sand flies and mosquitoes bit him. His head hurt.

Philip had seen the remains of Brown's campsite earlier in the day. He knew the bones must be close.

STOP AND THINK

Author's Craft Why does the author use short, choppy sentences on this page?

Philip was trying to find the location of *Albertosaurus* fossils shown in Brown's old photograph.

All alone, Philip climbed another hill. He stopped to hold up a photo. It looked just like the scene in front of him. He also could see that years ago someone had dug into the rock there. Philip had found Brown's bone bed!

Brown's photo was old, but Philip could see that the hills still looked the same.

Holes or cuts in rocky hills are clues that someone might have dug there before.

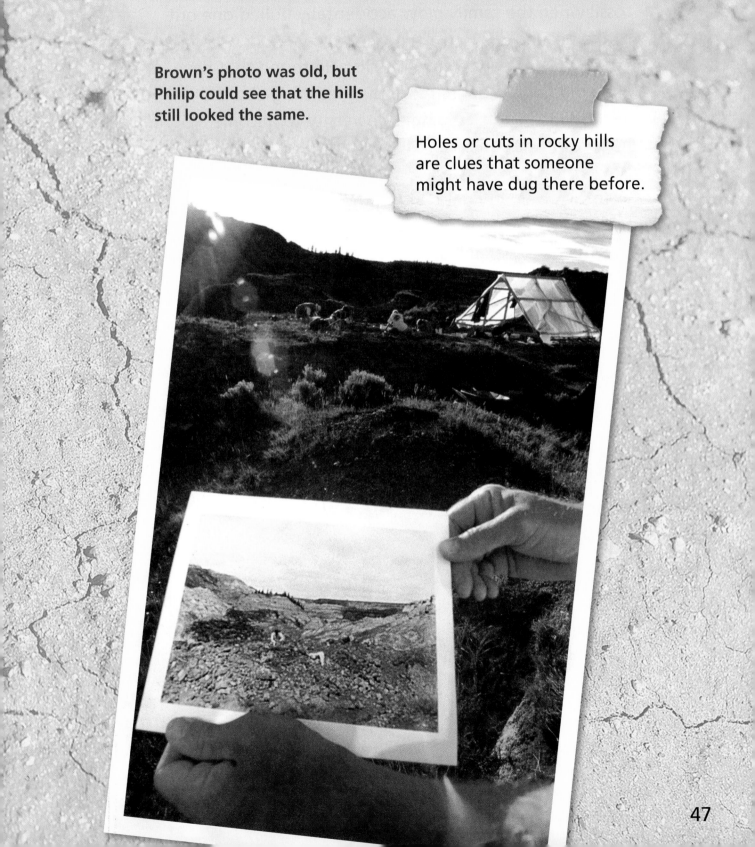

Barnum the Bone Hunter

Barnum Brown grew up in Kansas in the late 1800s. His family dug and sold coal. Young Barnum saw his first fossil when the family plow accidentally pulled one out of the ground.

Brown went on to study fossils. He found that he liked digging up bones more than learning about them in class. So he left Columbia University to become a bone hunter for the American Museum of Natural History in New York City.

Brown was very good at finding fossils. Henry Fairfield Osborn, the head of the museum, joked that Brown could "smell fossils." News writers called him "Mr. Bones."

At the American Museum of Natural History in New York City, Brown helped put together the bones he found.

Finding the First T. rex

In 1908, Brown found this *T. rex* skeleton. It can be
seen at the American Museum of Natural History.

In the early 1900s, Brown dug up *Tyrannosaurus rex*
(tuh ran uh SOHR uhs REKS) skeletons, first in Wyoming,
and later in Montana. These were the first *T. rex* skeletons
ever found.

For several years, Brown returned to Montana to dig
for fossils. The bones he found there were often stuck in
hard rock. He sometimes used dynamite to get them out.

Then in 1910 a terrible thing happened in Brown's
life. His wife died. Brown tried to forget his sadness by
hunting for more fossils. He rafted down Red Deer River
Canyon in Canada. He camped in the area, and looked for
bones. Soon, Brown made a surprising discovery.

Finding Many Meat-Eaters

In Canada, Brown found a place where many skeletons were buried. The skeletons belonged to *Albertosaurus*, a large meat-eating dinosaur. It was the first time anyone had found the bones of so many meat-eating dinosaurs in the same spot.

Brown dug up some of the bones. He wrote only a few lines about his find but didn't say how unusual it was. He didn't say why he thought so many individuals of the same species were together. He didn't tell what this discovery might mean.

The *Albertosaurus* bones were sent to the museum and put away. There they lay in a basement storage room for many years with other dinosaur fossils.

Albertosaurus got its name because the dinosaur's fossils were first found in Alberta, Canada.

A Fierce Family

Albertosaurus was part of a family of fierce, meat-eating dinosaurs called tyrannosaurids. Tyrannosaurus rex was also part of this family.

Albertosaurus was smaller than Tyrannosaurus rex, but it was strong. Albertosaurus could see and smell well. It had many sharp teeth. Its huge, powerful jaws could crush bone.

Like Tyrannosaurus rex, Albertosaurus lived and hunted alone. At least, that's what paleontologists thought. One man was about to change their thinking, however. He had some ideas about these ancient creatures.

> ✔ **STOP AND THINK**
>
> **Visualize** What words and phrases help you visualize how Albertosaurus looked and acted?
>
> **TEKS** 3.2B; 3.10

Tyrannosaurus rex was about 40 feet (12 meters) long. Albertosaurus was about 30 feet (9 meters) long.

Philip Currie's Question

In 1976, Philip Currie read what Brown wrote about the site full of albertosaurs. At that time, most paleontologists thought tyrannosaurids lived alone. If so, asked Philip, why were many of these animals buried together? Had they died together? Had they lived together?

Some plant-eating dinosaurs had lived in groups. Maybe some of the meat-eaters that hunted them did, too, thought Philip. After all, big groups of animals were hard to hunt alone. Maybe albertosaurs hunted in packs.

Philip was busy learning about many kinds of fossils and dinosaurs, however. He put his questions away for many years, just as Brown had put away his fossils.

Albertosaurus had about seventy teeth in its gigantic jaws.

The Bones in the Basement

◄ The American Museum of Natural History, where Brown's *Albertosaurus* fossils were stored.

This fossil foot bone from an *Albertosaurus* was first discovered by Barnum Brown in Alberta, Canada, and then rediscovered by Philip Currie in New York City. ▶

Philip thought about his questions again 20 years later. This time, however, something happened that made him hunt for answers.

Philip came across some *Albertosaurus* bones in the basement of the American Museum of Natural History—the museum where Barnum Brown had worked. He could tell that the bones were from the badlands in Canada where Brown had been searching for fossils.

Philip saw that Brown had found at least nine albertosaurs in one spot. He also saw that Brown had taken only a few bones from each animal. More bones were still buried in the badlands, waiting to be discovered.

The Bones in the Badlands

Place where Philip rediscovered the *Albertosaurus* fossil site first found by Barnum Brown

Philip discovered more than bones at the museum. He also found Brown's field notes and a photo of Brown's site. Using these clues, Philip was able to find the bone bed.

✔️ **STOP AND THINK**

Conclusions Why did finding so many albertosaur fossils in one place make the team believe that albertosaurs had lived together?

TEKS 3.13B

Locating the spot was just the first step, however. Philip and his team worked for months to dig out each fossil. At least 22 albertosaurs were buried in the rock.

After the work was done, a new question came up. Did finding many fossils together prove that the animals had lived, died, and even hunted as a group?

Philip uncovering *Albertosaurus* bones in the badlands

In the days of Barnum Brown, fossil hunters were not always able to keep good records. Today, paleontologists carefully record their finds with photographs, drawings, maps, and reports.

What May Have Happened

Philip knew there could be other reasons for the fossils being together. Many of these ideas only brought up more questions, however.

For example, the albertosaurs could have died in quicksand. Yet different kinds of dinosaurs could die in quicksand. Philip had found the fossils of only one kind—*Albertosaurus*.

Maybe the albertosaurs had gathered to lay eggs. If so, however, the fossils should have been about the same age and size. Yet Philip had found small, young animals as well as large, old animals.

Philip's hunt had ended. Yet he needed more evidence to show that the meat-eaters had lived together.

A reconstructed nest of fossilized dinosaur eggs

Scientists know that dinosaurs laid eggs because fossil eggs of several kinds of dinosaurs have been found.

More Groups of Meat-Eaters

Rodolfo Coria uncovers teeth on a huge dinosaur jawbone.

More evidence came when a paleontologist named Rodolfo Coria phoned Philip. Coria was calling from Argentina. He also had found a spot where a group of meat-eating dinosaurs was buried. So perhaps meat-eaters did live in groups after all.

Scientists found more places with groups of meat-eating dinosaurs. These places were all over—Arizona, Montana, South Dakota, Utah, Mongolia, and Zimbabwe.

Philip also looked carefully at the footprints of meat-eating dinosaurs in the Peace River Canyon of Canada. The footprints showed that meat-eating dinosaurs may have traveled together.

Digging Deeper

Did some meat-eating dinosaurs spend time living and hunting together? Scientists still aren't sure. They can only make smart guesses based on the fossils they have found.

Other questions are still unanswered as well. Why did the albertosaurs at Brown's site die? What killed so many animals at one time? A big storm? A forest fire?

Philip Currie says that a paleontologist is like a detective. The mysterious death happened millions of years ago. No one saw it. Using clues, the scientist tries to tell what happened, how, and why. As long as there are fossils waiting to be found, the investigation continues.

By studying fossils, experts can create models like this life-size *Albertosaurus*.

1. Which words from page 48 help the reader understand the meaning of <u>fossils</u>?

   ⬭ *grew up in Kansas*

   ⬭ *sold coal*

   ⬭ *digging up bones*

   ⬭ *left Columbia University*

2. ✔ **TARGET SKILL** **Conclusions**

   Phillip Currie searched for Brown's bone bed. What conclusion can you draw about Phillip Currie from reading about his experience? List facts to support your conclusion. Use a chart like this one. **TEKS** 3.13B **ELPS** 4J

3. ✔ **TARGET STRATEGY** **Visualize**

   Which graphics in the selection helped you visualize how big the dinosaurs were and what they looked like? **TEKS** 3.15B; 3.2C

4. **Oral Language** Work in pairs. Use the Retelling Cards to explain how Phillip Currie found the bone bed. Look at your partner while you speak. **TEKS** 3.30

   Retelling Cards

 TEKS **3.2C** establish reading purpose/monitor comprehension; **3.13B** draw/support conclusions; **3.15B** locate/use graphic features of text; **3.30** speak coherently/effectively about topics; **ELPS** **4J** employ inferential skills to demonstrate comprehension

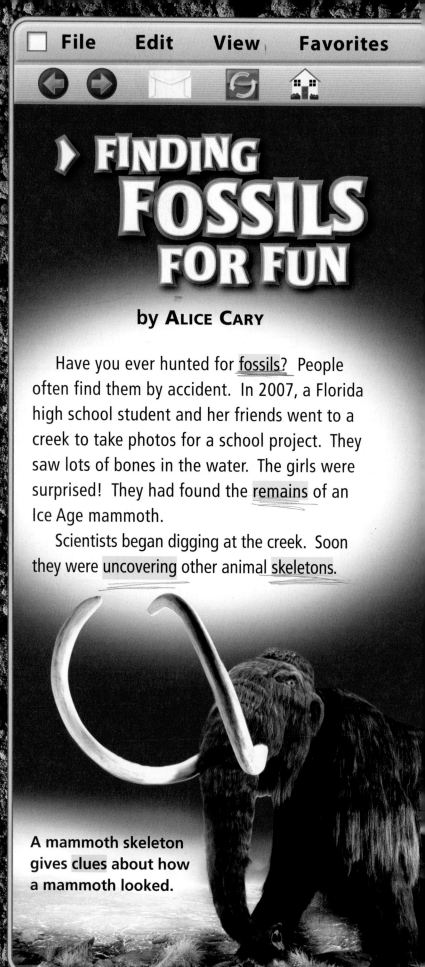

FINDING FOSSILS FOR FUN

by ALICE CARY

Have you ever hunted for fossils? People often find them by accident. In 2007, a Florida high school student and her friends went to a creek to take photos for a school project. They saw lots of bones in the water. The girls were surprised! They had found the remains of an Ice Age mammoth.

Scientists began digging at the creek. Soon they were uncovering other animal skeletons.

A mammoth skeleton gives clues about how a mammoth looked.

search

Fossils

Fossils are evidence of ancient life. Sometimes dirt or sand covers leaves and bones. Layers of dirt and sand protect these remains from damage. The layers build up as time passes. After many years, the remains harden and become fossils.

You may find fossils buried near you! The chart gives you tips for hunting them.

Hunting Guide

Where to Look	What to Hunt	Tools	Searching Tips
layers of rock	eggs, nests	hammer and chisel	Work carefully so you don't miss anything.
layers of sand or mud	footprints, leaf impressions	notebook, pen, camera	Take notes to keep track of where each discovery was found.
deserts, canyons, cliffs, hills, and mountains	shells	plastic box or newspapers and rubber bands for carrying finds	

Anyone Can Find Fossils!

You're never too young to find fossils. David Shiffler loved fierce dinosaurs. In 1995, when he was only three years old, David dug up a green rock. He called it a dinosaur egg.

David's father took the rock to a museum a few months later. David was right! He had found a piece of dinosaur egg! Scientists could prove it. The egg was about 150 million years old!

Hunt Fossils Safely

▷ **Take an adult.**
▷ **Choose a safe location.**
▷ **Get permission to hunt before you start.**
▷ **Wear safety glasses.**

COOL CLICKS!

Museums with Fossils

Fossils in the News

Fossil Finds

Making Connections

Text to Self   ELPS 5G

Be a Fossil Hunter After reading about people who hunt for fossils, do you think you'd like to be a fossil hunter? Write a paragraph explaining why or why not.

Text to Text   TEKS 3.15A; RC-3(E) ELPS 3D

Tell the Steps Work in pairs. Take turns telling the steps to take when you go fossil hunting, based on what you read in *The Albertosaurus Mystery* and "Finding Fossils for Fun." Make sure no steps are left out. Try to tell the steps in the correct order.

Text to World   TEKS 3.26C

Connect to Science Dinosaurs lived on Earth for about 150 million years! Scientists divide this time into the Triassic, Jurassic, and Cretaceous periods. Find out the dates of each of those periods, take notes, and then make a timeline to show what you found.

Pterosaurus

TEKS 3.15A follow/explain written directions; **3.26C** take notes/categorize evidence; **RC-3(E)** summarize information in text; **ELPS 3D** speak using content-area vocabulary; **5G** narrate/describe/explain in writing

Grammar

Articles The words *a*, *an*, and *the* are called **articles**. Use *a* and *an* with singular nouns. Use *a* before words that begin with a consonant sound. Use *an* before words that begin with a vowel sound. Use *the* before both singular and plural nouns.

Academic Language

article

Articles
Jess found a dinosaur bone.
He searched in an old cave.
I saw the bone yesterday.
The scientists at the museum want to see it, too.

Turn and Talk **Work with a partner. Read each group of words aloud. Decide which article may be used before each word.**

❶ (a, an) egg

❷ (the, an) kite

❸ (a, an) red hat

❹ (the, an) bumpy road

❺ (a, an) hour

❻ (a, an) angry bull

Word Choice Adjectives add details about people, places, and things. When you write, use exact adjectives so your reader can better picture what you are saying.

Less Exact Adjective	More Exact Adjective
big dinosaur	enormous dinosaur
some fossils	twenty fossils
old photo	ancient photo
good teeth	sharp teeth
local museum	American museum

Connect Grammar to Writing

As you revise your opinion paragraph, try to use exact adjectives.

Write to Persuade

☑ **Voice** The author of *The Albertosaurus Mystery* thinks fossil hunting is exciting. By sharing what really interests her, she gets her readers excited too. In your **opinion** paragraph, add ideas and details that will make your readers say, "Wow! I see what you mean!"

Rick wrote his opinion of studying prehistoric people. Later, he added more details to support his opinion.

Writing Traits Checklist

☑ **Ideas**
Did I explain my ideas clearly?

☑ **Organization**
Did I begin by telling my opinion?

☑ **Word Choice**
Did I use exact adjectives?

☑ **Voice**
Are my supporting reasons and details right for my audience?

☑ **Sentence Fluency**
Do my sentences flow smoothly?

☑ **Conventions**
Did I punctuate my sentences correctly?

Revised Draft

I love learning about prehistoric people. The way scientists study them is ~~interesting.~~ like solving a mysterious puzzle. Prehistoric people left no books about their lives. They just left objects that give clues. I am also amazed by how they got along without modern inventions. They lived in caves or huts, even in freezing weather. Imagine camping out for your whole life!

66

Amazing People from the Past
by Rick Yoshida

I love learning about prehistoric people. The way scientists study them is like solving a mysterious puzzle. Prehistoric people left no books about their lives. They just left objects that give clues. I am also amazed by how they got along without modern inventions. They lived in caves or huts, even in freezing weather. Imagine camping out for your whole life! They got all their food by hunting or finding plants. Don't you wonder what kids did for fun? There are lots of great facts to learn about prehistoric people.

> I added details that will make my opinion clear. I also used exact adjectives.

Reading as a Writer

What reasons support Rick's opinion best? Where can you add more persuasive details in your own paper?

67

Poems about Nature

A TREE IS GROWING

✓ TARGET VOCABULARY

pollen

store

clumps

passages

absorb

throughout

coverings

spines

tropical

dissolve

Vocabulary Reader

Context Cards

City Parks

 TEKS 3.4B use context to determine word meaning; **ELPS** 4D use prereading supports to comprehend texts

Vocabulary in Context

1 pollen

This bee carries pollen from flower to flower, which helps seeds grow.

2 store

A baobab tree can store, or keep, lots of water in its trunk.

3 clumps

The flowers on some trees grow in clumps, or bunches.

4 passages

A leaf has small passages, or tubes, that allow water to spread all over.

- **Study each** Context Card.
- **Make up a new context sentence using two Vocabulary words.**

5 absorb

A plant's roots absorb water. They soak it up.

6 throughout

Sap passes throughout a tree. It travels to every part.

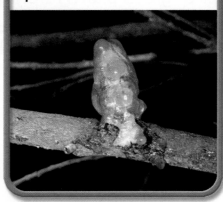

7 coverings

Different kinds of trees have different coverings, or outer layers.

8 spines

Many kinds of cacti are covered in sharp spines.

9 tropical

Some plants grow in warm, damp, tropical climates near the equator.

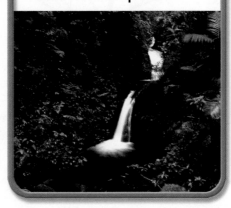

10 dissolve

If you add salt to water, it will dissolve, or mix, with the water.

Background

✓ TARGET VOCABULARY **Tree Talk** All trees have roots that absorb water. Minerals dissolve in that water. The water and minerals then travel through passages in the trunk. Some trees in dry climates have special trunks that help them store water. When a tree needs a drink, the stored water spreads throughout the branches. Tropical rain forests do not have this problem. Rain there is so plentiful, trees and giant clumps of green plants rarely go thirsty!

Trees have many different kinds of coverings. Some have spines for protection. Others have thick bark. Some trees have flowers, which produce pollen.

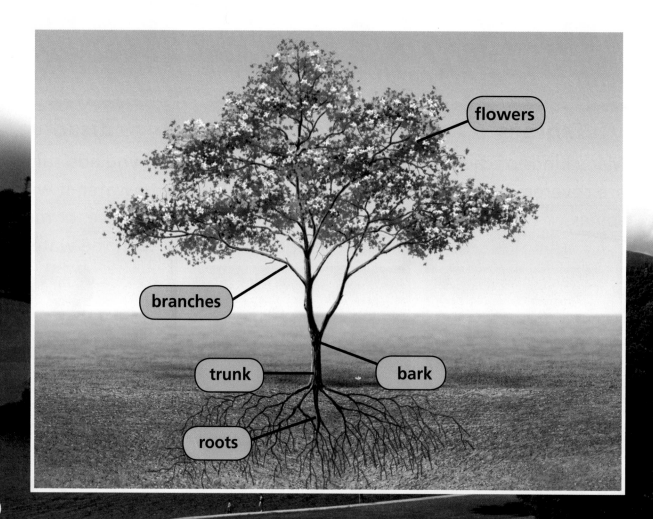

flowers

branches

trunk

bark

roots

TEKS **3.2B** ask questions/clarify/locate facts/details/use text evidence, **3.15B** locate/use graphic features of text; **RC-3(B)** ask questions of text; **RC-3(C)** monitor/adjust comprehension **ELPS** **4I** employ reading skills to demonstrate comprehension

Comprehension

✔ TARGET SKILL Text and Graphic Features

The author of *A Tree Is Growing* uses text and graphic features to make ideas about trees clear. Use a chart like this to list some features and the purpose of each feature.

Text or Graphic Feature	Page	Purpose

✔ TARGET STRATEGY Question

When you have a question or are confused about what you are reading, look for pictures, diagrams, or charts that show what the text describes. Ask yourself, *How can this text or graphic feature help me better understand what I am reading?*

✔ TARGET VOCABULARY

pollen	throughout
store	coverings
clumps	spines
passages	tropical
absorb	dissolve

✔ TARGET SKILL

Text and Graphic Features Tell how words and art work together.

✔ TARGET STRATEGY

Question Ask and answer questions before you read, while you read, and after you read to stay more focused on the text.

GENRE

Informational text gives factual information about a topic.

 TEKS RC-3(C) monitor/adjust comprehension; **ELPS** 4F use visual/ contextual/peer/teacher support to read/ comprehend texts

MEET THE AUTHOR
Arthur Dorros

Arthur Dorros loves trees. When he was five, he planted a maple seedling. The tree grew taller than a two-story house! The author believes that everyone has stories to tell. He encourages children all over the country to write.

MEET THE ILLUSTRATOR
S. D. Schindler

When S. D. Schindler was just four years old, he won a red wagon in a coloring contest. S. D. Schindler loves nature as much as he loves art. He used plants and animals from the woods near his home as models for the illustrations in *A Tree Is Growing*.

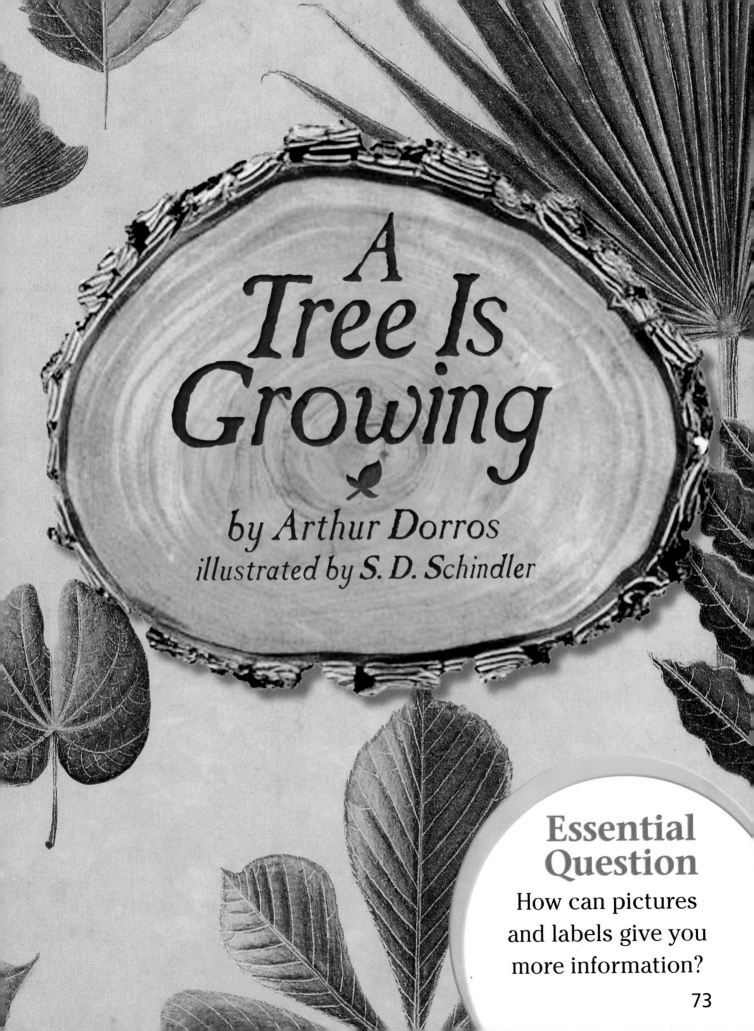

A Tree Is Growing

by *Arthur Dorros*

illustrated by *S. D. Schindler*

Essential Question

How can pictures
and labels give you
more information?

73

A giant tree may look as if it has always been big. But even the biggest tree keeps growing and changing.

In the spring you can see that a tree is growing as you watch buds on the branches unfold into leaves.

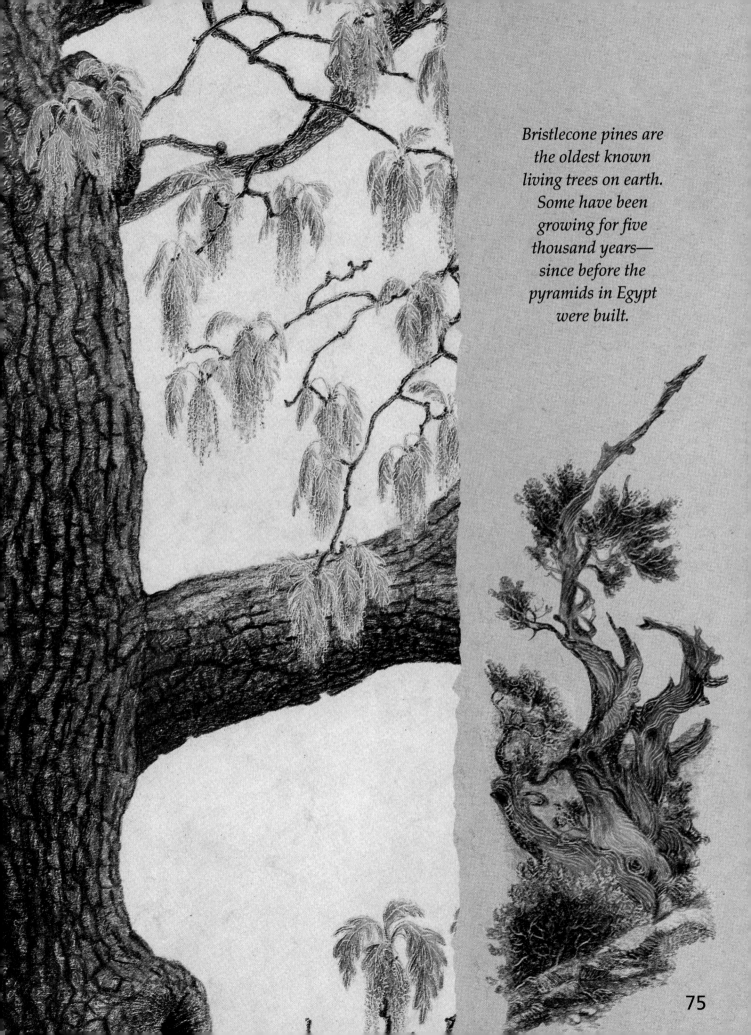

Bristlecone pines are
the oldest known
living trees on earth.
Some have been
growing for five
thousand years—
since before the
pyramids in Egypt
were built.

White oak

Palm

Gingko

Leaves can be skinny needles or big heart shapes. Whatever shape or size a leaf is, it makes food for the tree.

A kind of sugar is made in the leaves. Trees use the sugar as food.

Breadfruit tree

Empress tree

White pine

Red maple

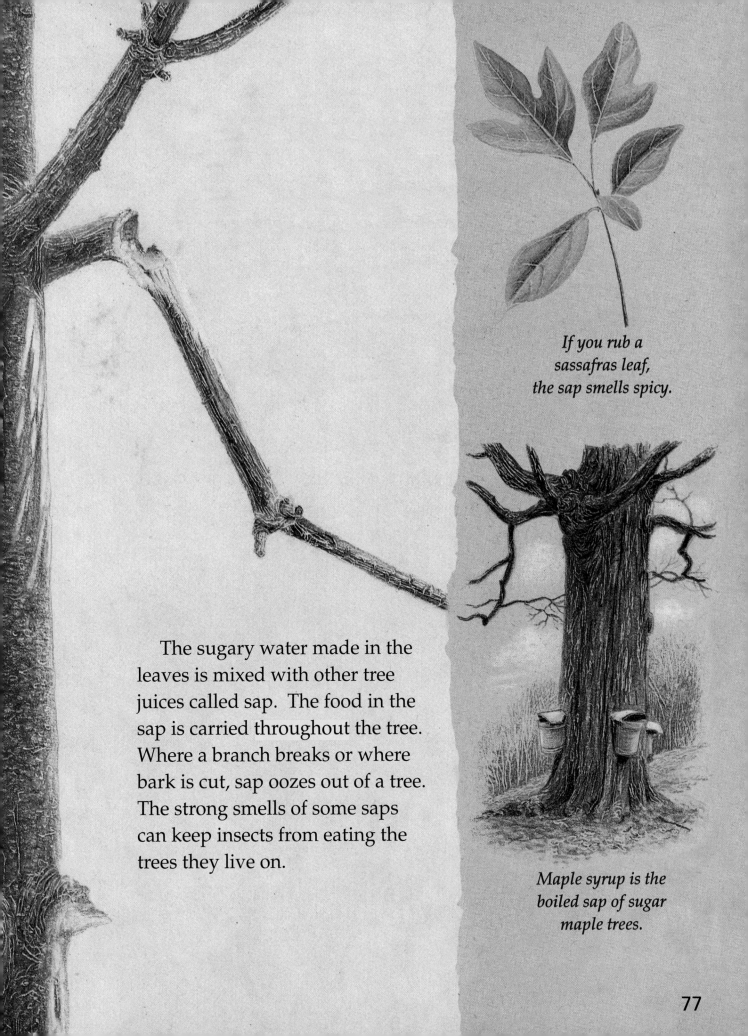

*If you rub a
sassafras leaf,
the sap smells spicy.*

The sugary water made in the leaves is mixed with other tree juices called sap. The food in the sap is carried throughout the tree. Where a branch breaks or where bark is cut, sap oozes out of a tree. The strong smells of some saps can keep insects from eating the trees they live on.

*Maple syrup is the
boiled sap of sugar
maple trees.*

Moth
caterpillar

Baobab trees store water in the trunks. When a baobab tree trunk is swollen with water, it is round and fat. In dry weather, the tree gets water from the trunk. Then the trunk gets thinner.

Water

A tree needs sunlight, air, soil, and water to grow.

Water travels through passages in the trunk and branches up to the leaves. The water moves up the trunk as if it is being sucked through a straw.

Sugary sap made in the leaves travels down other passages in the trunk, taking food to different parts of the tree.

✔ **STOP AND THINK**

Question What is shown in the diagram? Use the information in paragraph 2 to help you understand what is happening.

TEKS 3.2B, 3.15B; **ELPS** 4J

A few kinds of trees drop roots from branches into the soil to gather water. Banyan tree roots grow into columns all around the tree.

Growing roots are strong. A root can lift a sidewalk or split a rock as it grows. By splitting the rock, it helps make soil.

White oak

Earthworms

Beetle grub

The roots of a tree grow into the ground and hold the tree in place. Roots are like pipelines. They absorb water and carry it into the tree.

A tree's roots spread out far underground. They usually grow out a little farther than the tree's branches.

Trees need minerals to grow. Minerals are tiny particles that are found in the soil. Salt is one kind of mineral. Like salt, other minerals dissolve in water. They are mixed in with the water that roots absorb and are carried throughout the tree.

Mushrooms growing among the roots of a tree can help it get minerals. And the mushrooms and plants growing near a tree get water brought by the tree's roots.

Bicolored boletus
mushrooms

Flicker

Bark is the skin of a tree. The outer layer of bark protects the tree. When an oak tree is young, the bark is as smooth as a baby's skin. As the tree grows older, the bark becomes rough and cracked.

STOP AND THINK

Author's Craft How does the author help readers picture what oak tree bark is like when it is young and when it is old?

Polyphemus
moth

*Looking at the bark
of a tree can help
you know what
kind of tree it is.*

*The cork used for
bulletin boards is
the peeled-off
outer bark of a
cork oak tree.*

*Honey locust bark
has spines to help
protect the tree.*

In cool climates, cambium only grows in spring and summer. Count growth rings to see how old a tree was when it died. An old fir tree can have over a thousand rings, one for each year it lived.

In tropical rain forest trees, the cambium grows all year and there are no rings. It is hard to tell the ages of those trees.

Growth rings

Snail

Phloem

Cambium

Xylem

Underwing moth

The bark you can touch and see is not growing anymore. Underneath it is a layer of growing bark, called *cambium*. Each year's cambium growth is a ring in the wood of a tree. As trees add new cambium, the trees become bigger around.

Next to the cambium are two layers called *xylem* and *phloem*. Water from the roots moves through the xylem, and sap from the leaves moves through the phloem.

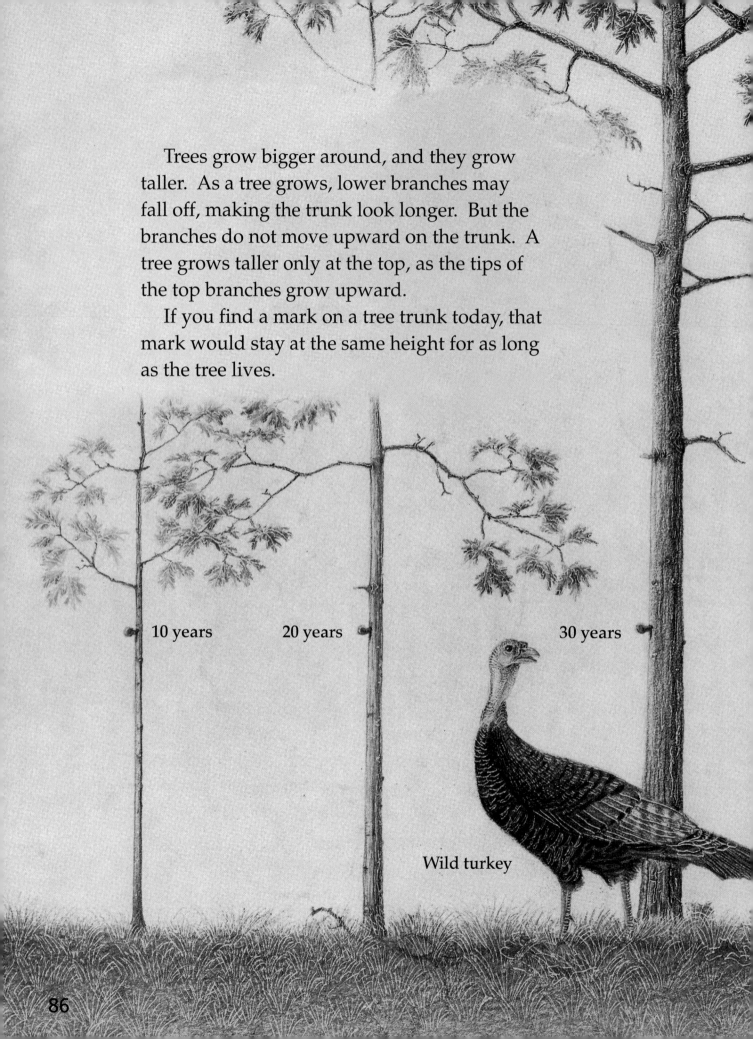

Trees grow bigger around, and they grow taller. As a tree grows, lower branches may fall off, making the trunk look longer. But the branches do not move upward on the trunk. A tree grows taller only at the top, as the tips of the top branches grow upward.

If you find a mark on a tree trunk today, that mark would stay at the same height for as long as the tree lives.

10 years

20 years

30 years

Wild turkey

50 years   200 years

Sequoias are some of the tallest trees in the world—over three hundred feet tall.

Catkins

Purple finch
(male)

Saucer
magnolia

Nectar-eating bat

Calabash tree

Birds, insects, and even bats are attracted to flowers to drink their sweet juices. When they brush the flowers, the animals get a powder called pollen on them. The animals carry the pollen to other flowers. When the pollen mixes with certain parts of the flowers, seeds grow. Wind also helps pollinate flowers.

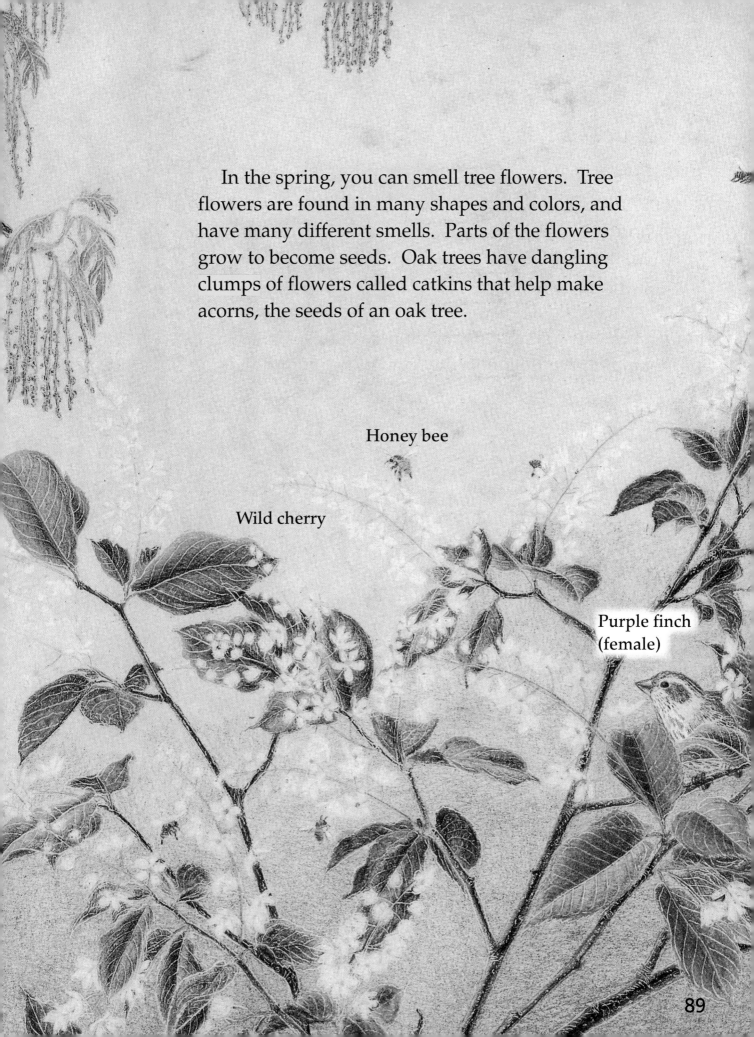

In the spring, you can smell tree flowers. Tree flowers are found in many shapes and colors, and have many different smells. Parts of the flowers grow to become seeds. Oak trees have dangling clumps of flowers called catkins that help make acorns, the seeds of an oak tree.

Honey bee

Wild cherry

Purple finch (female)

Sugar maple

An oak tree can drop more than fifty thousand acorns in one year. Only a few of them grow into oak trees. Most are eaten, are crushed, rot, or land in a place where they cannot take root.

Acorns can be carried away and dropped or buried by animals to grow in new places. Other kinds of seeds blow in the wind or float on water.

Sugar maple seed

Acorns

Gray
squirrel

Different kinds of trees
make seeds with
different coverings.
Nuts, cones, and fruits
all have seeds inside.

Brazil nut

Mountain
pine cone

Cherry

Coconuts are seeds of
a palm tree. A coconut
can float across the
ocean and sprout on a
sandy beach.

91

Autumn is a great time to collect leaves. Each tree has its own special color.

Tulip poplar

Gingko

Big-tooth aspen

Sweet gum

Pin oak

In cool climates, trees stop growing in autumn. The leaves of many trees stop making sugary food for the tree, and they lose their green color. Then you can see the red, brown, yellow, and orange colors that are also in the leaves.

Pine trees and some other trees have needles or leaves that do not change color in autumn.

Beetles

Earthworms

Spider

Millipede

92

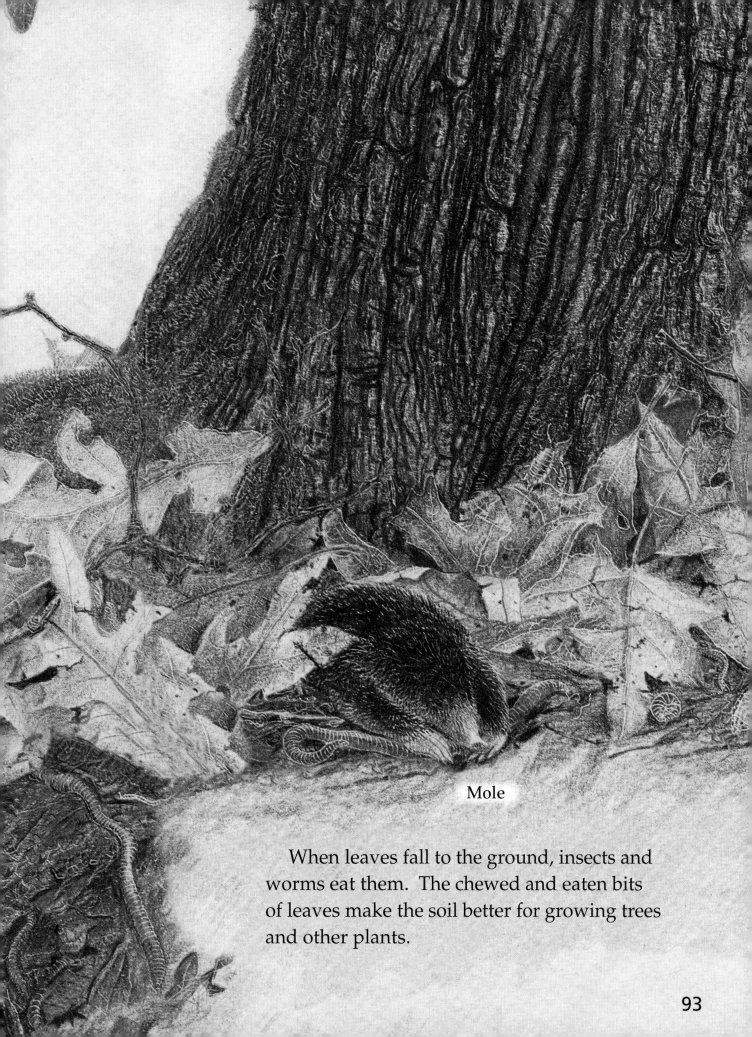

Mole

When leaves fall to the ground, insects and worms eat them. The chewed and eaten bits of leaves make the soil better for growing trees and other plants.

93

Trees rest in the cold of winter, and their branches are bare. They may look as if they are dead. But look closely and you can see small buds that will become leaves and flowers in the spring.

In the spring, listen to the wind rustling the leaves. The trees are growing again.

White oak

Horse chestnut

Your Turn

1. In this text, what does the word <u>store</u> mean?

   ◯ market

   ◯ use all at once

   ◯ keep for the future

   ◯ supplies

   TEKS 3.4B

2. ✔ **TARGET SKILL** **Text and Graphic Features**

   What information can you get from the graphic features in this selection? Use a column map like this to identify the purpose of each graphic feature. **TEKS** 3.15B

3. ✔ **TARGET STRATEGY** **Question**

   Find one place in *A Tree Is Growing* where you had a question about what you were reading. How did you answer your question? Now reread another text, "Tree Talk," on page 70. Clarify information about trees, using both texts. **TEKS** 3.2B

4. **Oral Language** Work with a partner. Use the Retelling Cards to retell the important facts from *A Tree Is Growing*. **ELPS** 4G

   Retelling Cards

TEKS **3.2B** ask questions/clarify/locate facts/details/use text evidence; **3.4B** use context to determine word meaning; **3.15B** locate/use graphic features of text; **ELPS** **4G** demonstrate comprehension through shared reading/retelling/responding/note-taking

GENRE

Poetry uses the sound and rhythm of words to show images and express feelings.

TEXT FOCUS

Personification gives human traits to objects, animals, and plants. Discuss which human characteristics are given to the sea and the mountains in these two poems. Say which words make them look, feel, and sound like people.

TEKS **3.6** describe forms of poetry/how they create imagery; **3.10** identify sensory language; **3.31** participate in discussions/ build on others' ideas

Poems About
Nature

The poems you will read next are about nature. What is the mood, or feeling, of each poem? Which words or rhythms help create this mood?

Until I Saw the Sea

Until I saw the sea
I did not know
that wind
could wrinkle water so.

I never knew
that sun
could splinter a whole sea of blue.

Nor
did I know before,
a sea breathes in and out
upon a shore.

by Lilian Moore

Fog coverings may hide a mountaintop completely. The mountain appears to dissolve into the gray mist.

Mountain Mist

tender
breath
of mountains

playful
steam
clouding

the windows
of the village
bakery

the golden
eyeglasses
of my father

the windshield
of my family's
station wagon

as we cross
Mexico's western
mountain range

by Francisco X. Alarcón

From high to low tide, the ocean's depth can change by up to fifty feet! As the tide goes down, the water carves narrow passages in the sand.

Knockabout and Knockaboom

Mohave Desert
Southwestern United States

The wind that whistles desert songs
　　By spinning tops of sand
Leaves behind a silent sea
　　Of dune-upon-dune land.

The Land of Sand turns hot as fire,
　　But once or twice a year
Into the picture of a sky
　　Two thunderclouds appear.

They knockabout and knockaboom
　　To make a THUNDERSHOWER!
And when they leave, they always leave
　　At least . . . one desert flower.

by J. Patrick Lewis

Like other deserts throughout the world, the Mojave Desert is dry. When rain falls, desert plants absorb as much water as they can. A large saguaro cactus can store nearly a ton of water in its spines! If spring brings enough rainfall, clumps of bright flowers appear. Bees buzz from blossom to blossom, collecting pollen. For a short while, the desert looks almost lush and tropical!

Write a Nature Poem

Write your own nature poem. Try including personification.

Making Connections

Text to Self

A Tree and Me In what ways are you like a tree? In what ways are you different? Work in a small group. Take turns telling things you have in common with a tree, and ways you are different.

Text to Text

Write a Poem Choose your favorite poem from *Poems About Nature*. Then write your own poem in a similar style about a tree included in *A Tree Is Growing*. Use words that help the reader see, hear, smell, and feel the tree.

Text to World

Connect to Science Research a local tree at the library. Inspect this type of tree in person. Take notes about the tree. Write a paragraph that gives important facts about the tree. Then draw a picture to go with your paragraph.

TEKS **3.10** identify sensory language; **3.18B** write poems that convey sensory details; **3.26A(i)** collect information from surveys/inspections/interviews ; **3.26A(ii)** collect information from experts/reference texts/online searches; **3.26C** take notes/categorize evidence; **3.29A** listen/ask questions/make comments ; **ELPS 3G** express opinions/ideas/feelings

Grammar

Using the Verb *be* and Helping Verbs The verbs *am*, *is*, *was*, *are*, and *were* are forms of the verb *be*. They do not show action. They tell what someone or something is or was.

Academic Language

helping verbs

Subject	Present	Past
I	am	was
you	are	were
he, she, it	is	was
singular noun *(Thomas)*	is	was
plural noun *(trees)*, we, they	are	were

Sometimes the words *has* and *have* help other verbs to show past time. *Has* and *have* are called **helping verbs**.

Subject	Helping Verb
he, she, it	He has watched the trees grow.
I, you, we, they	They have grown very tall.

 Try This! **Write each sentence correctly using the verb that best completes each sentence.**

1. I (is, am) a great tree climber.

2. The girls (has, have) picked apples.

3. They (was, were) at the orchard yesterday.

Sentence Fluency When two sentences have the same predicate, you can put the sentences together. Join the two subjects and use the word *and* between them. You may have to change the forms of the verbs *be* and *have* to go with their subjects.

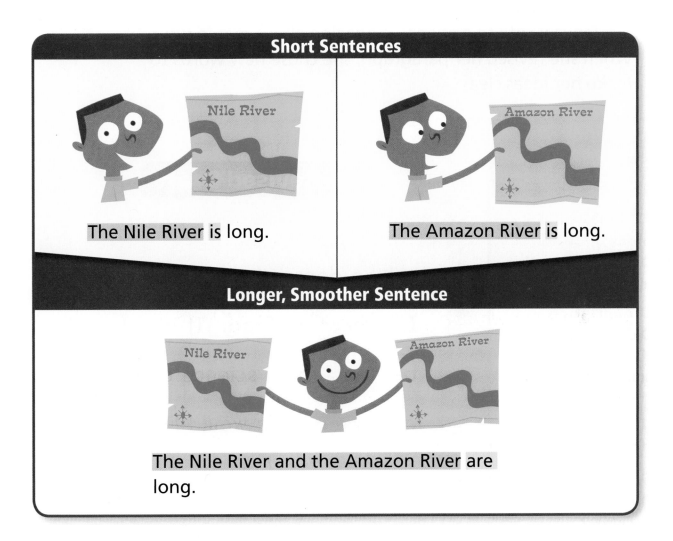

Short Sentences

The Nile River is long.

The Amazon River is long.

Longer, Smoother Sentence

The Nile River and the Amazon River are long.

Connect Grammar to Writing

As you revise your persuasive essay, try to combine subjects to make longer sentences. Change the verb form to make it go with the subject.

Write to Persuade

✅ **Word Choice** In *A Tree Is Growing*, the author writes that tree bark "becomes rough and cracked." As you revise your **problem and solution paragraph**, try to use exact words, too.

Tanya wrote to a science magazine about maple syrup. When she revised her paragraph, she chose new words to make her ideas clear.

Writing Traits Checklist

☑ **Ideas**
Did I use supporting ideas and examples?

☑ **Organization**
Did I clearly state the problem and solution?

☑ **Word Choice**
Did I use clear, exact words?

☑ **Voice**
Do I sound sure of my ideas?

☑ **Sentence Fluency**
Did I use both simple and compound sentences?

☑ **Conventions**
Did I write neatly in cursive script?

Revised Draft

Who doesn't love maple syrup? It's great on ~~food~~ waffles and pancakes. It also would be ~~good~~ an interesting subject for a science article. I am sure people would ~~like~~ enjoy reading about it.

The Next Science Article
by Tanya Petrov

Who doesn't love maple syrup? It's great on waffles and pancakes. It also would be an interesting subject for a science article. I am sure people would enjoy reading about it.

Maple syrup is made from the sap of sugar maple trees. The article could tell about the journey from inside the tree to inside the refrigerator. It could also tell how people discovered maple syrup and how they made it in the past. Both students and scientists could learn about this natural treat.

> I added some exact words. I also combined two sentences to avoid repeating a predicate.

Reading as a Writer

Why did Tanya replace "food" with "waffles and pancakes"? Where can you add more exact words in your own paper?

✓ **TARGET VOCABULARY**

fiery

within

horrifying

ancient

mysterious

emergency

panicking

scientific

prehistoric

immediately

Vocabulary   Context
Reader   Cards

ELPS 3D speak using content-area vocabulary

Vocabulary in Context

1 fiery
After this fiery building has cooled, rescue dogs may go inside to help.

2 within
Within seconds, this helper dog finds and pushes the right button.

3 horrifying
This dog is used to the deep snow. He does not find it horrifying, or scary.

4 ancient
Ancient art from Roman times proves people kept dogs as pets long ago.

- Study each Context Card.
- Tell a story about two or more pictures, using Vocabulary words.

5 mysterious

This dog is sniffing at a mysterious package to help guess what it holds.

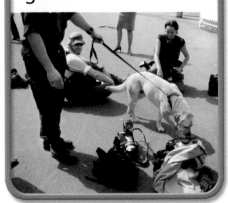

6 emergency

A rescue dog can help an emergency team find trapped people quickly.

7 panicking

Herding dogs can help guide scared, or panicking, animals.

8 scientific

People do scientific research to create new medicines that can help sick dogs.

9 prehistoric

Dogs helped people hunt in prehistoric times, which were very long ago.

10 immediately

As soon as the light changes, this dog immediately walks forward.

Background

✓ **TARGET VOCABULARY** **The Power of Volcanoes** People have lived with volcanoes since prehistoric times. Ancient cultures found volcanoes mysterious. They thought they were alive! When fiery lava within the volcano erupted, people thought the volcano was angry. It was horrifying!

Today, scientific facts explain why volcanoes erupt. Active volcanoes are checked daily. A warning is given before an eruption can cause an emergency situation. People can leave the area immediately without panicking, and lives are saved.

Scientists are careful when they study lava, which is nearly 2000 degrees! When lava cools, it hardens into rock. That's how the Hawaiian Islands formed.

Comprehension

✔ **TARGET SKILL** **Cause and Effect**

In *Dogzilla*, some events cause other events to happen.
The first event is the cause. The second event is the effect.
Use a chart like this one to identify causes and effects as
you read.

Cause	Effect

✔ **TARGET STRATEGY** **Summarize**

You can use the causes and effects from your chart
to summarize, or retell, the most important events in
Dogzilla. This will help you understand what you read.

Main Selection

MEET THE AUTHOR AND ILLUSTRATOR

Dav Pilkey

Warning: *Dogzilla* is rated EG for "Extremely Goofy." Ever since he was eight years old, Dav Pilkey has been making extremely goofy books. To create illustrations for *Dogzilla*, Pilkey first took photos of his dog Leia and his pet mice Flash, Rabies, and Dwayne. Then he cut the animals out of the photos and pasted them onto backgrounds that he had painted. By the way, Pilkey's first name is pronounced just like Dave.

DOGZILLA

written and illustrated by
DAV PILKEY

Essential Question

How can one event lead to a series of adventures?

It was summertime in the city of Mousopolis,

and mice from all corners of the community had come together to compete in the First Annual Barbecue Cook-Off.

As the cook-off got under way, smoke from the hot grills lifted the irresistible scent of barbecue sauce over the rooftops of the city.

A gentle wind carried the mouth-watering smell into the distance, right over the top of an ancient crater. Before long, a strange and mysterious sound was heard: "Sniff . . . sniff. Sniff . . . sniff sniff sniff sniff . . ."

All at once, the volcano began to tremble.
And suddenly, up from the very depths of the earth
came the most terrifying creature ever known to mousekind:
the dreadful Dogzilla!

STOP AND THINK

Cause and Effect What events take place that cause Dogzilla to come out of the volcano? What do you predict will happen next?

TEKS 3.2A

115

Immediately, soldiers were sent out to stop the mighty beast. The heroic troops were led by their brave commanding officer, the Big Cheese.

"All right, you old fleabag," squeaked the Big Cheese, "get those paws in the air—you're coming with us!"

Without warning, the monstrous mutt breathed her horrible breath onto the mice.

"Doggy breath!" screamed the soldiers. "Run for your lives!"

"Hey, come back here," shouted the Big Cheese to his troops. "What are you, men or mice?"

"We're MICE," they squeaked.

"Hmmmm," said the Big Cheese, "you're *right*! . . . Wait for me!"

The colossal canine followed the soldiers back to
Mousopolis, licking up all of the food in her path.
Afterward, Dogzilla wandered through the city
streets, doing those things that come naturally to dogs.
Dogzilla chased cars—right off the freeway!

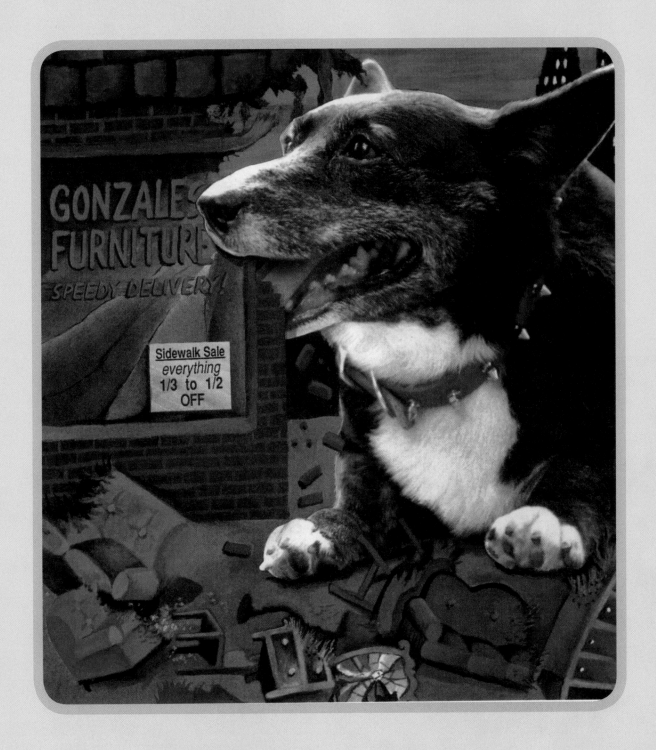

Dogzilla chewed furniture—and the furniture store as well. And Dogzilla dug up bones—at the Museum of Natural History.

Meanwhile, the Big Cheese had organized an emergency meeting with one of the city's greatest scientific minds, Professor Scarlett O'Hairy.

"Gentlemice," said Professor O'Hairy, "this monster comes from prehistoric times. It is perhaps millions of years old."

"Maybe we could teach it to do something positive for the community," suggested the Big Cheese.

"I'm afraid not," said Professor O'Hairy. "You simply can't teach an old dog new tricks!

"If we're going to defeat this dog, we've got to *think* like a dog! We've got to find something that *all* dogs are afraid of—something that will scare this beast away from Mousopolis FOREVER!"

"I've got an idea," squeaked the Big Cheese . . .

STOP AND THINK

Author's Craft Which details does the author use in the words and pictures to make the mice seem like people?
ELPS 4F

Dogzilla \ˋdôg· zi· lə\ *noun*
1: a big, hairy dog   2: of, or relating to a big, hairy dog
adv. 3: big, hairy dogishness
[< P Latin   *Ogzilladay*]

Within minutes, the mice had assembled at the center of town.

"All right, Dogzilla," shouted the Big Cheese, "no more Mister Mice Guy—it's BATHTIME!"

Suddenly, a blast of warm, sudsy water hit Dogzilla with tremendous force.

The panicking pooch let out a burst of hot, fiery breath, and the chase was on!

The Big Cheese tried to catch up to the hot dog with all the relish he could muster.

Dogzilla hightailed it out of town, and back into the mouth of the ancient volcano.

"Well, I'll be dog-goned," squeaked the Big Cheese. "It worked!"

With the horrifying memory of the bubble bath etched in her mind forever, Dogzilla never again returned to Mousopolis.

✔ STOP AND THINK

Summarize Summarize the ways in which Big Cheese and his troops respond to Dogzilla's attack on Mousopolis.
TEKS 3.8A

Within a year, Mousopolis had rebuilt itself . . . just in time for the Second Annual Barbecue Cook-Off. The mice of Mousopolis fired up their grills, confident that they would never see or hear from Dogzilla again.

However, there was one thing they hadn't counted on . . .

Puppies!

Your Turn

1. Which word on page 113 means the opposite of <u>new</u>?

   ⬭ *gentle*

   ⬭ *ancient*

   ⬭ *strange*

   ⬭ *mysterious*

   TEKS 3.4C

2. ✔ **TARGET SKILL** **Cause and Effect**

   Use a chart like this to name two causes and two effects of the Big Cheese's emergency meeting. **TEKS** 3.2B **ELPS** 4K

3. ✔ **TARGET STRATEGY** **Summarize**

   Use causes and effects to sequence and summarize how the mice got rid of Dogzilla. **TEKS** 3.8A

4. **Oral Language** With a partner, use the Retelling Cards to act out a scene from the story. Try to speak clearly and with expression. **TEKS** 3.30

Retelling Cards

 TEKS **3.2B** ask questions/clarify/locate facts/details/use text evidence; **3.4C** identify/use antonyms/synonyms/homographs/homophones; **3.8A** sequence/summarize main events/influence on future events; **3.30** speak coherently/effectively about topics; **ELPS** **4K** employ analytical skills to demonstrate comprehension

Whose Land Is It?
by Ellen Gold

✓ **TARGET VOCABULARY**

fiery	emergency
within	panicking
horrifying	scientific
ancient	prehistoric
mysterious	immediately

GENRE

Informational text gives factual information about a topic. This is a newspaper feature article.

TEXT FOCUS

Photographs show true pictures of important text details. **Captions** explain about these photos. Look at the photos and captions before you read to predict what the article will be about. After you read, say if your predictions were correct.

 TEKS **3.2A** use ideas to make/confirm predictions; **3.13D** use text features to locate information/make and verify predictions; **3.15B** locate/use graphic features of text; **ELPS** **4.D** use prereading supports to comprehend texts

TODAY'S

Monday, September 5, 2010

Whose Land Is It?

by Ellen Gold

People and Wild Animals

People and animals need places to live. Animals have lived in the wilderness for thousands of years. They live in ancient forests, oceans, and other habitats. Yet wild animals also live in people's yards. They live in cities, too!

Coyotes are no strangers to cities. One even walked into a restaurant in Chicago! Within moments, a panicking worker had climbed onto the counter.

NEWS

Community	Classifieds
Third Graders	**Looking for a**
Meet the Mayor	**new pet?**

FROM THE PAGES OF
WEEKLY READER

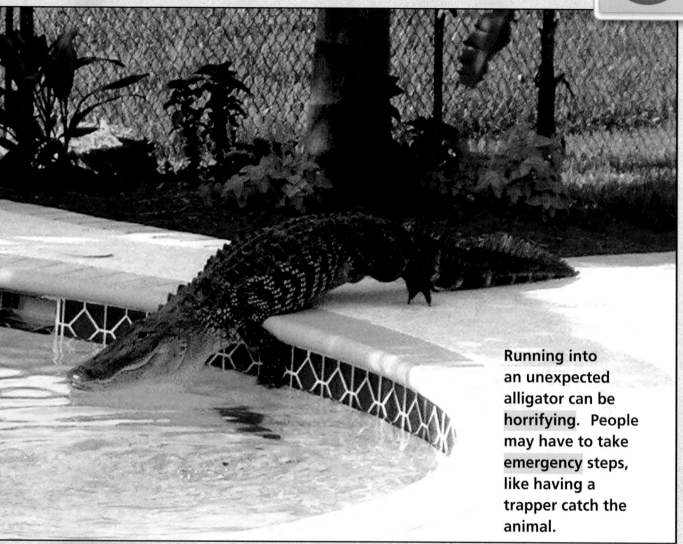

Running into an unexpected alligator can be **horrifying**. People may have to take **emergency** steps, like having a trapper catch the animal.

Habitat Loss

Why are wild animals moving closer to people? They are losing their habitats. Then they must find new places to live. Fires destroy many animals' homes. Some years are especially fiery. In 2006, fires burned nearly 10 million acres of wild land in the United States.

People destroy habitats, too. People build homes, stores, and roads where wild animals live. In Florida many homes are near swamps and waterways. These are places where alligators live.

Continued from page 129

Changing Ways

Alligators have been around since prehistoric times. They mostly fear people. Yet that may be changing. Why is this?

The reason is far from mysterious. Some people feed alligators. Then those alligators stop fearing people. They may think that all people will feed them.

Other animals link people to food, too. Scientific experts know a lot about black bears. Country bears look for food during the day. City bears eat at night. They know that people put out garbage. So, city bears find food in dumpsters and trashcans.

How can people keep bears away? People need to change their habits. They should use bear-proof trashcans. They should fasten the cans immediately after use. If bears can't get food, they won't come back.

This black bear has wandered into someone's backyard garden, right in the heart of a big city! Have wild animals ever visited your home?

Making Connections

Text to Self

Connect to Art Think about a time you had a funny, scary, or interesting experience with an animal. Draw a picture to show what happened.

Text to Text

ELPS 3E, 4G

People and Animals In *Dogzilla*, the dog is the scary creature who causes danger to the mice. In "Whose Land Is It?," both animals and people cause danger to each other. How? With a partner, discuss how both animals and people can seem scary to each other.

Text to World

TEKS 3.21 ELPS 5G

Connect to Science *Dogzilla* is a funny story about a dog, but "Whose Land Is It?" explains that where animals live is a serious issue. Write an essay to convince the reader that people should live cooperatively with wild animals. Include details from the text to support your point.

TEKS 3.21 write persuasive essays; **ELPS** 3E share information in cooperative learning interactions; 4G demonstrate comprehension through shared reading/retelling/responding/note-taking; 5G narrate/describe/explain in writing

131

Grammar

Irregular Verbs Some verbs have a special spelling to show past time. They have another spelling when used with *has, have,* or *had*.

Academic Language

irregular verb

Present	Past	with *has, have,* or *had*
go	went	has, have, had gone
see	saw	has, have, had seen
do	did	has, have, had done
run	ran	has, have, had run
come	came	has, have, had come

 Work with a partner. Read the sentences aloud. Choose the correct verb for each sentence.

❶ The dog (come, came) to Mousetown for food.

❷ He had (saw, seen) a barbeque.

❸ He ate everything there, and now he has (ran, run) away.

❹ The mice have (came, come) together to talk.

❺ The mice (did, done) not know what to do!

132

Word Choice When you write, it is important to use exact verbs. Your readers will understand your writing better.

Less Exact Verb	Exact Verb
The mice ran away from the giant dog.	The mice dashed away from the giant dog. The mice darted away from the giant dog. The mice scampered away from the giant dog.

Connect Grammar to Writing

As you revise your persuasive essay next week, look for places where you can use exact verbs.

Reading-Writing Workshop: Prewrite

Write to Persuade

☑ **Ideas** When you plan a **persuasive essay**, picture your audience asking, "Why should I do what you want?" Draw a cartoon to explore your reasons. Later, you can organize your ideas in a persuasion chart.

Daniel wanted to persuade children to join a club. He explored his reasons in the cartoon below. Then he organized his ideas in a chart.

Writing Process Checklist

▶ **Prewrite**

☑ **Did I think about my purpose?**

☑ **Did I choose a goal I really care about?**

☑ **Did I make my position clear?**

☑ **Did I give reasons that will persuade my audience?**

☑ **Did I order my reasons?**

Draft

Revise

Edit

Publish and Share

134

Persuasion Chart

My Goal: Children should join the Penguin Club.

Reason: It's fun and interesting!

Details: learn cool facts
go to Science Museum
live penguins at the Aquarium

Reason: Penguins need help.

Details: fewer places to live
dogs hunt penguins
oil spills

Reason: You'll meet new people.

Details: kids are nice and love animals
meet our leader, Mr. Spears

> I picked my best reasons and chose an order for them. Then I added details.

Reading as a Writer

Which details would persuade you to join Daniel's club? What details can you add to your own chart to persuade your readers?

✓ TARGET VOCABULARY

shelter

colony

constant

wilderness

climate

region

unexpected

gliding

overheated

layer

Vocabulary
Reader

Context
Cards

 TEKS 3.4E alphabetize to third letter/ use dictionary/glossary; **ELPS** 4D use prereading supports to comprehend texts

Vocabulary in Context

1 shelter

A tent can make a good shelter for an explorer. It is a good place to keep warm.

2 colony

Some people take trips to study a colony, or large group, of penguins.

3 constant

Steady, or constant, rain can make hiking trails slippery and difficult to use.

4 wilderness

Explorers often travel through wilderness, or unsettled areas.

- **Study each Context Card.**

- **Place the Vocabulary words in alphabetical order.**

5 climate

Boaters must avoid ice when exploring regions with a very cold climate.

6 region

This overgrown jungle is in a hot and rainy region, or area.

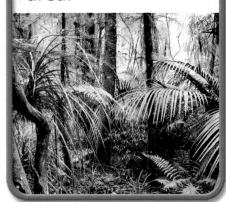

7 unexpected

The view from the top surprised these hikers. It was quite unexpected.

8 gliding

Gliding along, or flying by wind power, is an exciting way to explore.

9 overheated

Smart explorers find shade and drink water when they feel overheated.

10 layer

A layer of ice must be several inches thick before it is safe to cross.

Background

✔ TARGET VOCABULARY **Life in Antarctica** Would you like to visit the bottom of the world? The region around the South Pole in Antarctica is a frozen, empty wilderness. However, scientists from around the world live and work there in a busy colony. They study the Earth's climate.

Temperatures can sink to −100°F, so scientists must be careful outside the warmth of their shelter. Gliding on skis over a thick layer of snow and ice, they watch for unexpected, deep cracks. One thing is certain here, though. They're unlikely to get overheated!

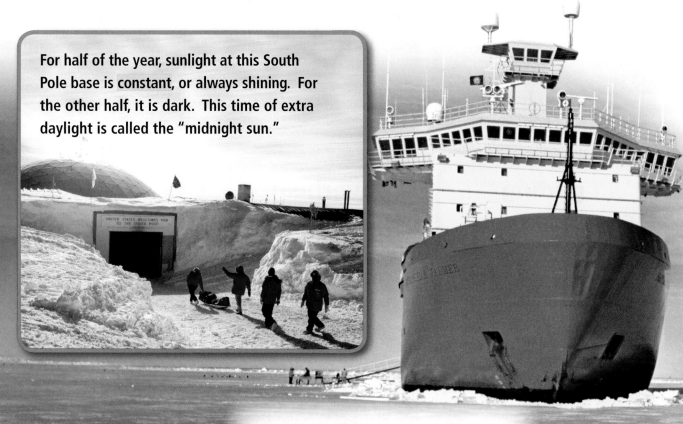

For half of the year, sunlight at this South Pole base is constant, or always shining. For the other half, it is dark. This time of extra daylight is called the "midnight sun."

Bow of icebreaker in ice in McMurdo Sound with Adélie Penguins (*pygoscelis adeliae*) walking by

Comprehension

✔ TARGET SKILL Main Ideas and Details

The author of *Life on the Ice* gives important information, or main ideas, about Antarctica. Details in the text help make each main idea clear. As you read, use a chart like this one to show how the details support the main ideas.

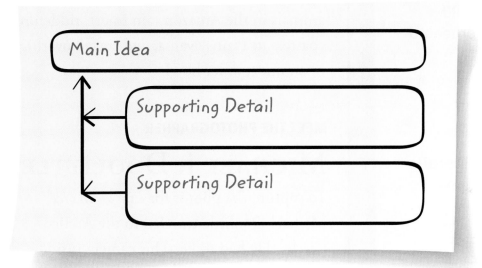

Main Idea

Supporting Detail

Supporting Detail

✔ TARGET STRATEGY Infer/Predict

Think about the main ideas and details on your chart. Use them to infer, or figure out, more about living and working in Antarctica.

LIFE on the ICE

SUSAN E. GOODMAN
photographs by MICHAEL J. DOOLITTLE

✔ TARGET VOCABULARY

shelter	region
colony	unexpected
constant	gliding
wilderness	overheated
climate	layer

✔ TARGET SKILL

Main Ideas and Details
Tell important ideas and details about a topic.

✔ TARGET STRATEGY

Infer/Predict Use clues to figure out more about the selection.

GENRE

Informational text gives factual information about a topic. Skim *Life on the Ice* before you read and predict what it will be about.

TEKS 3.13D use text features to locate information/make and verify predictions

MEET THE AUTHOR

SUSAN E. GOODMAN

Susan Goodman's life as a writer has taken her on some exciting adventures. She has gone swimming with dolphins in Florida, made friends with animals in the Amazon rain forest, ridden roller coasters in Pennsylvania, and stayed overnight in an underwater hotel.

MEET THE PHOTOGRAPHER

MICHAEL J. DOOLITTLE

To capture the photos for *Life on the Ice*, Michael Doolittle traveled to the Arctic Circle. He had to keep his camera inside his heavy coat to prevent it from freezing. Doolittle has collaborated with Susan Goodman on many books, including the whole *Ultimate Field Trip* series.

LIFE on the ICE

by SUSAN E. GOODMAN
with photographs by MICHAEL J. DOOLITTLE

Essential Question

Where are main ideas often found in nonfiction text?

The top and the bottom of our planet are covered with ice. The top, the Arctic, is home to the North Pole. It can be so cold that a cup of hot water, thrown in the air, will explode into a cloud of ice particles.

The North Pole is located in the middle of the Arctic Ocean and is usually covered by ice.

The South Pole is at the bottom of our planet on the continent of Antarctica. This region is even colder than the Arctic, sometimes plunging to –125°F (–87.2°C). In winter, parts of the oceans surrounding Antarctica freeze over, doubling its size. Antarctica is the coldest, driest, windiest place on Earth. It is so isolated that no human had even seen this continent until two hundred years ago.

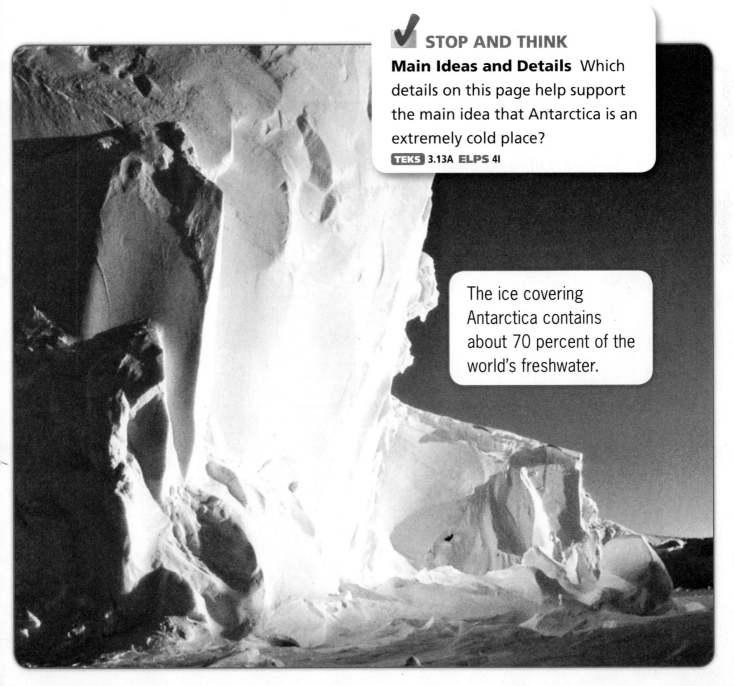

✔ **STOP AND THINK**

Main Ideas and Details Which details on this page help support the main idea that Antarctica is an extremely cold place?

TEKS 3.13A **ELPS** 4I

The ice covering Antarctica contains about 70 percent of the world's freshwater.

Places this cold, this extreme, are hard to imagine. In fall the sun sets and doesn't rise again for the entire winter. Months later, it shines twenty-four hours a day—all summer long.

Even though they are covered by ice, these regions are deserts—dry like the Sahara. Very little snow falls in either place. But when it does, it rarely melts. Over time, the snow becomes ice—in some places, almost three miles (5 km) thick.

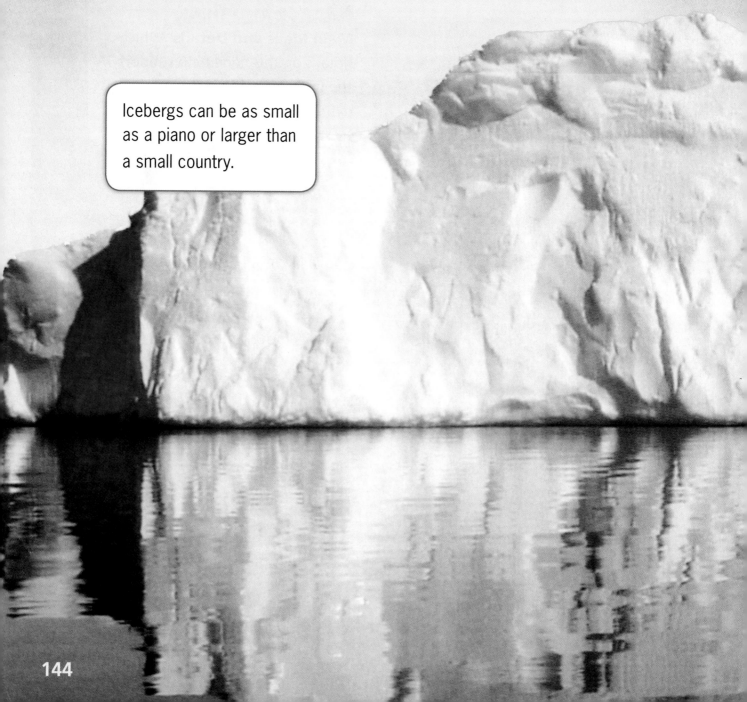

Icebergs can be as small as a piano or larger than a small country.

This ice is slowly moving, inching from the middle of the Arctic and Antarctica to their coasts. By the time pieces break off into the ocean and become icebergs, the ice is 100,000 years old.

People fly thousands of miles to reach the Poles. And when the winds kick up and blow the snow around, it's hard to know where the sky ends and the land begins. Pilots say that it's like flying inside a Ping-Pong ball.

Many of the instruments normally used to guide planes won't work there. In fact, navigators flying to the Poles are the only ones left in the U.S. Air Force who still help map their route with the stars. This is some of the hardest flying there is.

STOP AND THINK

Author's Craft What do the pilots mean when they say that flying in the Poles is like flying inside a Ping-Pong ball?

TEKS 3.10 **ELPS** 4F

Planes do not land in these wintry worlds by rolling down concrete runways. They use skis instead. And they slide like giant sleds until they stop. Gliding along, the skis get so hot that they melt the snow they're resting on. Pilots must pull them up when the planes stop. Otherwise, the wet snow would refreeze on the skis and the planes would be stuck to the ground.

When pilots land at the South Pole, they keep their engines running. It's so cold that they might not start up again.

It sounds like an adventure story, doesn't it? It *is* an adventure story—one with science. Scientists are today's explorers, braving the wilderness to learn more about our world.

The snow near the North Pole, for example, hasn't melted since the last ice age. Over 100,000 years of it has been pressed into an ice sheet almost 2 miles (3.2 km) thick. But each layer looks separate, like the rings of a tree.

Some scientists use this snow to measure air pollution. Others are drilling through this ice to pull out history. Each sample they bring up tells a story about the time when it was formed. Scientists have found volcanic ash from Italy's Mount Vesuvius, for instance, and pollution from ancient Roman times.

Scientists began this experiment to learn more about how ice ages begin and end. Before, they thought our climate needed thousands of years to change. Now they know it can happen much, much faster.

At the South Pole some scientists search for meteorites, rocks from outer space. Meteorites are no more likely to fall there than anywhere else on Earth. But, as one scientist explains, if you want to find something dark, it's easier to look on a big white sheet. His team has given thousands of meteorites to our space agency, the National Aeronautics and Space Administration (NASA), for study.

The Antarctic sky is a perfect window to the stars, the best on this planet. It is very clear because it's so cold and dry—and has a night that is six months long. Some scientists use telescopes to study the age of the universe. Others fly balloons to measure rays coming in from outer space.

At the Poles people wear many layers of clothing to keep warmth in and wind out. They wear big boots and overalls called fat-boy pants. Their mittens have furry backs to wipe their noses and warm their ears.

They also wear goggles. Without them, their eyes would get sunburned and temporarily blinded by the strong light bouncing off the snow.

No wearing rings, earrings, or sunglasses with metal frames in the extreme cold. Metal gets so cold that it will freeze any skin that it touches.

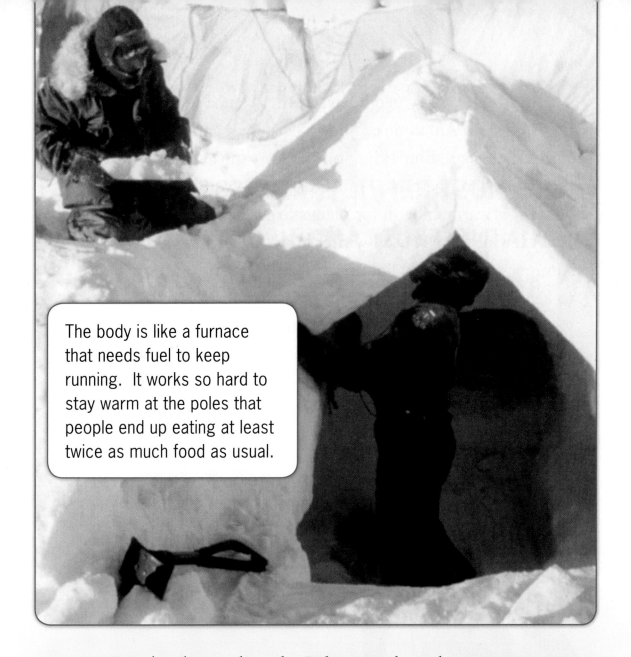

The body is like a furnace that needs fuel to keep running. It works so hard to stay warm at the poles that people end up eating at least twice as much food as usual.

People who work at the Poles must learn how to survive being stuck outdoors. On an unexpected "camping trip," they first build a quick shelter to get out of the wind. Then they build a better one and pack in close to one another, using body heat to stay warm.

Building shelters—doing any work—is much harder in extreme cold. Mittens are very bulky, but it's unsafe to go bare-handed for long. Getting too cold is dangerous, but so is getting overheated. Sweat can freeze into a layer of ice next to your body.

In summer many people live at the science stations in the Arctic and Antarctica. They have a gym and videos and spend their spare time skiing on the icy runways. But mostly they work hard, getting as much done as possible while the weather is warm enough for planes to fly in and out.

A few of them stay all winter long. Scientists say that summer's constant daylight tricks your body into wanting to keep going without rest. But in winter's endless darkness, you feel tired much of the time. One scientist even studies the people who winter-over at the South Pole. He wants to know what kind of person works well in such a small, isolated group. Someday his findings may help pick the people to live in a colony on Mars.

✔️ **STOP AND THINK**

Infer/Predict From the description of the Arctic or Antarctica, what can you infer about living on Mars?

TEKS RC-3D

Unlike most refrigerators, the one containing fruit and vegetables at the South Pole is heated.

154

In spring in Antarctica, the temperature finally climbs up to +10°F (−10°C) and it's warm enough for planes to fly in again. The scientists are eager to get on board and return to the colors and smells of the "green world." Once they buckle up, there is one last frosty problem to solve. The airplane must go 100 miles (160 km) per hour to take off, no easy task when sliding over ice. Sometimes pilots must travel 2 miles (3 km) to reach that speed. And sometimes they need extra help. Then they turn to the eight rockets attached to their plane.

A flick of the switch, a burst of flames and speed,
and they are on their way home.

Your Turn

1. Which words on page 153 help the reader know what <u>unexpected</u> means?

   ⬭ *stuck outdoors*

   ⬭ *quick shelter*

   ⬭ *pack in close*

   ⬭ *stay warm*

   ELPS 3F

2. ✓ **TARGET SKILL** **Main Idea and Details**

   What is the main idea about Antarctica on page 146? What details support the main idea? Use a chart like this to write supporting details.
   TEKS 3.13A; ELPS 4I

3. ✓ **TARGET STRATEGY** **Infer/Predict**

   How do you think the pilots will feel as they try to land at the Poles? Which details help you figure this out? **TEKS 3.13B; RC-3(D)**

4. **Oral Language** Use the Retelling Cards to tell a partner or the class facts about Antarctica. Try to speak clearly and avoid mumbling.
   TEKS 3.30

   Retelling Cards

 TEKS **3.13A** identify details/facts that support main idea; **3.13B** draw/support conclusions; **3.30** speak coherently/effectively about topics; **RC-3(D)** make inferences/use textual evidence; **ELPS 3F** ask/give information in various contexts; **4I** employ reading skills to demonstrate comprehension

Traditional Tales

The Raven:
an Inuit Myth

✔ TARGET VOCABULARY

shelter	region
colony	unexpected
constant	gliding
wilderness	overheated
climate	layer

GENRE

A **myth,** like this Readers' Theater, is a story that tells what a group of people believes about the world.

TEXT FOCUS

The **plot** in a myth may explain why or how something in nature came to be. After you read, tell in your own words what this myth explains. Give story details that describe how this natural thing came to be.

 TEKS 3.2B ask questions/clarify/locate facts/details/use text evidence; **3.5A** paraphrase themes/details of tales; **ELPS 4G** demonstrate comprehension through shared reading/retelling/responding/note-taking

Readers' Theater

The Raven:
An Inuit Myth

retold by Peter Case

Cast of Characters

Narrator	Person
Old Man	Raven

Narrator: Long ago, the People lived in darkness. There was no sun to help things grow. The People called to Raven for help.

Person: Oh, Raven, help us. Our lives are a constant struggle.

Raven: I have heard of an Old Man who has two glowing globes of light. I will try to get these globes.

Narrator: Raven went gliding over the dark wilderness. He came to the shelter where the Old Man lived with his daughter. There, Raven turned himself into a human child.

Old Man: I have a grandson! How wonderful!

Narrator: Raven spoke in the voice of a small child.

Raven: May I please play with the globes of light?

Old Man: Here, grandson, you can play with them.

Narrator: Raven thought of a trick to steal the globes. He pretended he was overheated inside the warm shelter.

Raven: It's so hot inside. I want to take the globes outside.

Old Man: Yes, grandson. You can play outside with the globes.

Narrator: Once Raven was outside, he put on his layer of feathers and flew off with the globes.

159

Narrator: When he got back to the colony of People, Raven threw the globes up into the sky. One became the sun and the other became the moon. The People were overjoyed.

Person: Now the climate will be good for growing food in this region of the world. Thank you, Raven, for the gift of the sun and for the unexpected gift of the moon.

Making Connections

Write a Story Imagine that you are a scientist in Antarctica. Write a short story that tells about your adventures there. Be sure that the story includes details about characters and setting, and an exciting ending that solves a problem in the story.

Discuss Texts Why is the sun so important to the scientists at the Poles and the people in *The Raven*? Talk about this issue in a small group. Listen carefully to one another. Ask each other questions.

Connect to Art The art in *The Raven* makes the action in the story more interesting. Look at how the style fits the story. Choose a part of *Life on the Ice* that you like. Make an illustration to go with that passage. Use a style that makes sense for the text.

 TEKS **3.18A** write imaginative stories; **3.29A** listen/ask questions/make comments; **3.31** participate in discussions/build on others' ideas; **RC-3(D)** make inferences/use textual evidence; **RC-3(F)** make connections between texts; **ELPS 2D** monitor understanding of spoken language/seek clarification; **5G** narrate/describe/explain in writing

TEKS 3.23C(i) recognize/use apostrophes in contractions/possessives; 3.24F spell complex contractions; ELPS 5E employ increasingly complex grammatical structures in writing

Grammar

Contractions You know that a **contraction** is a word made by putting two words together. An apostrophe replaces the letter or letters that are left out.

Academic Language

contraction

Two Words	Contraction
is not	isn't
have not	haven't
will not	won't
cannot	can't
I am	I'm
she is	she's
they are	they're
you will	you'll
he has	he's
should have	should've

 Try This!

Write the contraction for each of the words below.

❶ are not

❷ did not

❸ we are

❹ he will

❺ they have

❻ it is

Conventions When you write, use contractions.
This will make your writing more interesting to read.

Without a Contraction	With the Contraction *n't*
Even in the coldest months, penguins do not leave Antarctica.	Even in the coldest months, penguins don't leave Antarctica.

Without a Contraction	With Pronoun and Verb Contraction
I am wondering if scientists get gloomy during Antarctica's dark winter.	I'm wondering if scientists get gloomy during Antarctica's dark winter.

Connect Grammar to Writing

As you edit your persuasive essay, make sure you have written contractions correctly.

TEKS **3.17C** revise drafts; **3.20A(iii)** use concluding statement in brief compositions; **3.21** write persuasive essays; **3.22A(viii)** use/understand transitions; **3.23D** use correct mechanics

Reading-Writing Workshop: Revise

Write to Persuade

✔ **Organization** A **persuasive essay** explains reasons in detail. To help readers follow along, each reason has its own paragraph, starting with transition words, such as "Another reason…"

Daniel drafted his essay about joining a club. Later, he separated his reasons into paragraphs and added transition words.

Writing Process Checklist

Prewrite

Draft

▶ **Revise**

✔ Did I begin by telling my goal?

✔ Did I give strong reasons?

✔ Did I support my reasons with details and examples?

✔ Do my new paragraphs use transition words?

✔ Did I sum up my reasons in a concluding statement?

Edit

Publish and Share

Revised Draft

Do you love penguins? If your answer is yes, join the Penguin Club! ¶ The main reason to join is that It's fun and interesting. We visit the penguin exhibit at the Science Museum, see live penguins at the Aquarium, and do projects. You'll learn lots of cool penguin facts. For example, did you know that penguins go sledding on their stomachs?

The Penguin Club Is Cool!

by Daniel Singh

Do you love penguins? If your answer is yes, join the Penguin Club!

The main reason to join is that it's fun and interesting. We visit the penguin exhibit at the Science Museum, see live penguins at the Aquarium, and do projects. You'll learn lots of cool penguin facts. For example, did you know that penguins go sledding on their stomachs?

Another great reason to join the club is that penguins need your help. In some parts of the world, penguins have fewer safe, healthy places to live because of changes caused by people.

> I began a new paragraph for each reason. I was also careful to write contractions correctly.

Reading as a Writer

Why did Daniel divide his essay into paragraphs? In your paper, where should you divide your writing into paragraphs?

Read both selections. Then read the questions that follow them. Decide which is the best answer to each question.

Why We Have Winter: A Zuni Folktale

The Zuni are a Native American people of New Mexico and Arizona. Animals and nature are an important part of Zuni stories. This folktale explains how winter came to be.

1   Long ago, the land was always dark, and the weather was always warm. During that time, Eagle and Coyote often went out together to hunt for food. Eagle and Coyote enjoyed the warm weather outside when they hunted. However, hunting in the dark was difficult.

2   While hunting one day, Eagle and Coyote came to the home of the Kachinas. The Kachinas were powerful people who had a box that shined brightly. The Kachinas guarded the box closely. They never opened it.

3   When Eagle and Coyote saw the box, they had an idea. "If we had the box," said Coyote, "we could use the shining light to help us hunt in the dark."

4   "Let's wait until the Kachinas have gone to sleep," said Eagle. "Then we can take the box and run away."

5   Eagle and Coyote waited. Soon the Kachinas fell asleep. Coyote kept watch while Eagle swooped down and grabbed the box.

6   Eagle and Coyote were happy. The box made hunting in the dark much easier. As they hunted, Coyote thought about the box. What made the box shine so brightly? Coyote decided that he must see what was inside the box, but he had a problem. Eagle had not let go of the box since they had stolen it. Coyote thought of a plan.

7   "Eagle, my good friend," said Coyote. "Why not let me carry the box for a little while? You must be getting tired of clutching it all day long in your talons."

8   "No, no," said Eagle. "I can carry it. It's no trouble at all."

9   A little while later, Coyote asked again to carry the box. Once again, Eagle refused. Coyote did not give up. Every few minutes, he offered to carry the box. Coyote was so persistent that Eagle finally gave in. At last Coyote had his chance to peek inside the box!

10   As soon as Eagle turned his head, Coyote tipped open the lid just a little bit. Out flew the sun. Coyote was so startled that he did not even think about trying to catch it. The sun quickly flew far off in the sky.

11   With one small act, Coyote changed life for everyone on the planet. The sun never returned to the box. It stayed in the sky and gave heat and light to the land below. But because the sun had flown so far away, the land got much less heat than before. Now the land has light, but it is colder for part of every year. That time is called winter.

Reasons for the Seasons

Each student in Ashley's science class was asked to explain something in nature. Ashley wrote the following report.

1   Depending on where you live, seasons can mean different things. In Dallas, where we live, summer can be scorching. Winter here is not as cold as it is in some places, but it's always cooler than summer.

2   Have you ever wondered why Earth has winter, spring, summer, and fall? Our four seasons happen for two major reasons. One is the tilt of the Earth on its axis. The second is because of Earth's orbit around the sun.

3   Texas is in the Northern Hemisphere. That's the part of Earth that is north of the equator. The Northern Hemisphere includes the United States, Canada, and Mexico.Climates of the Northern Hemisphere are mostly different from those of the Southern Hemisphere. One hemisphere has the colder weather of winter while the other hemisphere has the warmer weather of summer.

GO ON

4   Why does this happen? As Earth orbits around the sun, different parts of Earth tilt toward the sun at different times of year. When the Northern Hemisphere tilts toward the sun, we have summer. When the Northern Hemisphere tilts away from the sun, we have winter.

> **Use "Why We Have Winter: A Zuni Folktale" and "Reasons for the Seasons" to answer questions 1–4.**

1   In paragraph 9 of "Why We Have Winter," which words help the reader know what the word <u>persistent</u> means?

   ⬭ *a little while later*

   ⬭ *did not give up*

   ⬭ *gave in*

   ⬭ *had his chance*

2   What is different about the two selections?

   ⬭ Only "Why We Have Winter" tells about the sun.

   ⬭ Only "Reasons for the Seasons" tells about summer.

   ⬭ Only "Why We Have Winter" tells a made-up story.

   ⬭ Only "Reasons for the Seasons" tells about seasons.

3   Read the diagram below and then answer the question that follows.

Why We Have Winter
• Folktale
• _____

• Gives an explanation

Reasons for the Seasons
• Science article
• Gives facts

Which of these goes on the blank line?

   ⬭ gives facts

   ⬭ tells why coyotes are persistent

   ⬭ has events that could not happen in real life

   ⬭ proves that Earth used to be dark all the time

4   How are Coyote from "Why We Have Winter" and Ashley from "Reasons for the Seasons" similar?

   ⬭ They both want to explain the seasons.

   ⬭ They are both real.

   ⬭ They are both sneaky.

   ⬭ They are both curious.

STOP

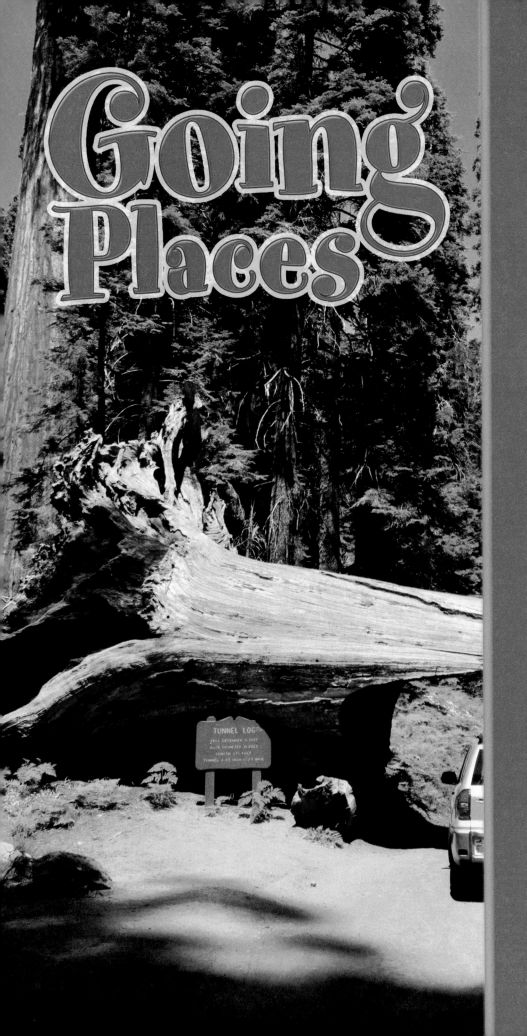

Going Places

Unit 5

Big Idea

There are many reasons to take a journey.

Paired Selections

Poems About Bugs

TWO BAD ANTS
CHRIS VAN ALLSBURG

✔ **TARGET VOCABULARY**

scout

narrow

surrounded

underground

puzzling

glassy

violently

liquid

soggy

unaware

Vocabulary Reader

Context Cards

World of Ants

TEKS 3.4B use context to determine word meaning; **ELPS** 1D speak using learning strategies

Vocabulary in Context

1 **scout**
This scout explores ahead of the others to lead the way.

2 **narrow**
In narrow spaces, explorers must walk in a single line to get through.

3 **surrounded**
This island is surrounded by water. You need a boat to get there.

4 **underground**
Exploring these underground caves means going down into the earth.

- **Study each Context Card.**

- **Make up a new context sentence that uses two Vocabulary words.**

5 puzzling

This street sign is so puzzling, or confusing, that drivers may get lost.

6 glassy

The surface of this lake is smooth and glassy. It reflects the boat like a mirror.

7 violently

If the wind blows too violently, the tree could blow down.

8 liquid

It's smart to bring lots of liquid, such as water, on a long hike.

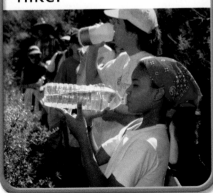

9 soggy

Food and clothing get wet and soggy when campers are caught in the rain.

10 unaware

The bear looks unaware of the people. It acts as if no one is there.

Background

✔ **TARGET VOCABULARY** **Ant Life** Watching a line of ants disappear underground can be puzzling. Where do they go?

Ants live in narrow, linked tunnels called colonies. Each ant has a job to do. The queen lays eggs. She is surrounded by soldier ants. They violently defend their busy home from attack. Worker ants dig tunnels. Outside the tunnel, scout ants search for food. Ants store food in special chambers, or rooms. This keeps the food from getting soggy if rain or another liquid floods their home.

tunnel

scout ant

food chamber

soldier ant

queen ant

worker ant

eggs

Ant Colony

Some ants live between glassy walls in an ant farm. They seem unaware of humans watching their community in action. How many kinds of ants are shown here?

Comprehension

✔ TARGET SKILL   Story Structure

Pay attention to the setting and the characters in *Two Bad Ants*. Then use story details to identify the plot. What problem do the characters face, and how do they find a solution? Show the story structure in *Two Bad Ants* in a story map like this one.

Problem	Events
Solution	

✔ TARGET STRATEGY   Monitor/Clarify

In *Two Bad Ants*, the author tells what story characters *think* is happening, not what is *really* happening. Readers must figure out story events on their own. When story events are confusing, try reading the text again or read ahead to figure out what is really happening to the ants.

TWO
BAD
ANTS

CHRIS VAN ALLSBURG

✔ TARGET VOCABULARY

scout	glassy
narrow	violently
surrounded	liquid
underground	soggy
puzzling	unaware

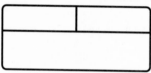
✔ TARGET SKILL

Story Structure Name the setting, character, and plot in a story. Say whether the story is told in the first or third person.

✔ TARGET STRATEGY

Monitor/Clarify As you read, find a way to clear up what doesn't make sense.

GENRE

A **fantasy** is a story that could not happen in real life.

 TEKS 3.8C identify narrator as first/third person;

MEET THE AUTHOR AND ILLUSTRATOR

Chris Van Allsburg

One morning Chris Van Allsburg came downstairs in his Rhode Island home to find two ants on the kitchen countertop. He began to imagine the strange journey the little insects might have made from his backyard to his kitchen. That is how Van Allsburg got the idea for *Two Bad Ants*.

Several of Van Allsburg's books, including his two Caldecott Medal winners, *Jumanji* and *The Polar Express*, have been made into movies.

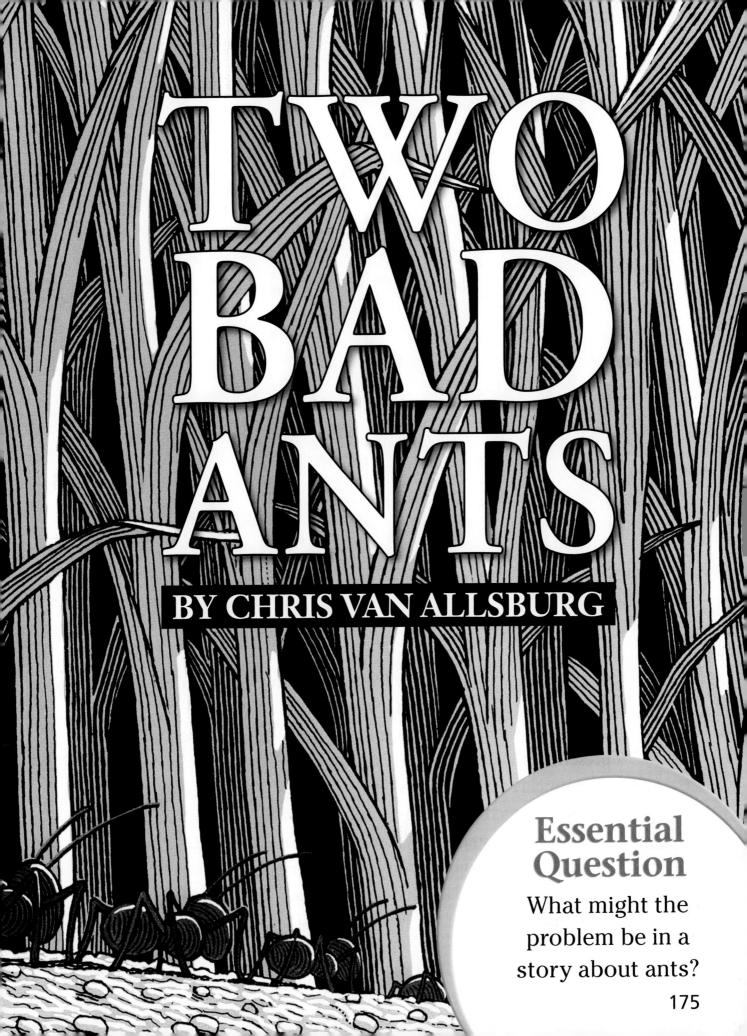

TWO BAD ANTS

BY CHRIS VAN ALLSBURG

Essential Question

What might the problem be in a story about ants?

175

The news traveled swiftly through the tunnels of the ant world. A scout had returned with a remarkable discovery—a beautiful sparkling crystal. When the scout presented the crystal to the ant queen she took a small bite, then quickly ate the entire thing.

She deemed it the most delicious food she had ever tasted. Nothing could make her happier than to have more, much more. The ants understood. They were eager to gather more crystals because the queen was the mother of them all. Her happiness made the whole ant nest a happy place.

It was late in the day when they departed. Long shadows stretched over the entrance to the ant kingdom. One by one the insects climbed out, following the scout, who had made it clear—there were many crystals where the first had been found, but the journey was long and dangerous.

They marched into the woods that surrounded their underground home. Dusk turned to twilight, twilight to night. The path they followed twisted and turned, every bend leading them deeper into the dark forest.

More than once the line of ants stopped and anxiously listened for the sounds of hungry spiders. But all they heard was the call of crickets echoing through the woods like distant thunder.

Dew formed on the leaves above. Without warning, huge cold drops fell on the marching ants. A firefly passed overhead that, for an instant, lit up the woods with a blinding flash of blue-green light.

At the edge of the forest stood a mountain. The ants looked up and could not see its peak. It seemed to reach right to the heavens. But they did not stop. Up the side they climbed, higher and higher.

The wind whistled through the cracks of the mountain's face. The ants could feel its force bending their delicate antennae. Their legs grew weak as they struggled upward. At last they reached a ledge and crawled through a narrow tunnel.

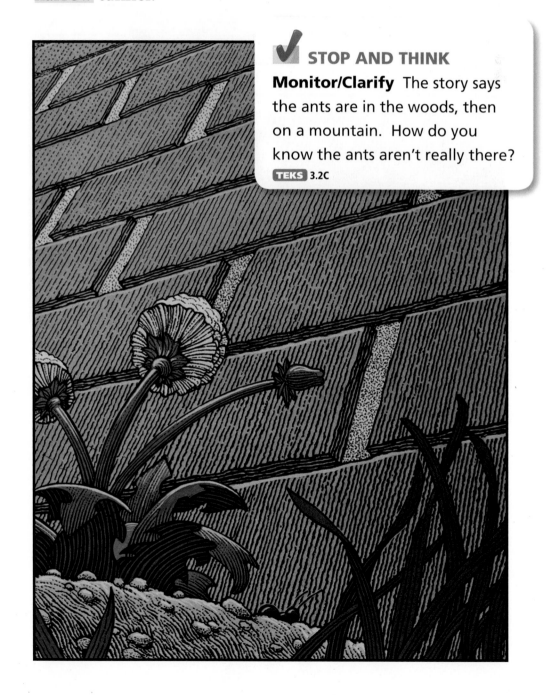

✔ **STOP AND THINK**

Monitor/Clarify The story says the ants are in the woods, then on a mountain. How do you know the ants aren't really there?

TEKS 3.2C

When the ants came out of the tunnel they found
themselves in a strange world. Smells they had known all
their lives, smells of dirt and grass and rotting plants, had
vanished. There was no more wind and, most puzzling of
all, it seemed that the sky was gone.

They crossed smooth shiny surfaces, then followed
the scout up a glassy, curved wall. They had reached their
goal. From the top of the wall they looked below to a sea
of crystals. One by one the ants climbed down into the
sparkling treasure.

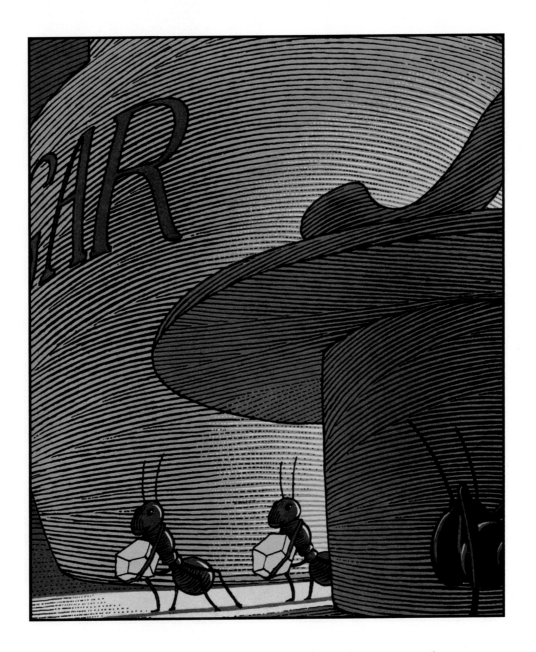

Quickly they each chose a crystal, then turned to start the journey home. There was something about this unnatural place that made the ants nervous. In fact they left in such a hurry that none of them noticed the two small ants who stayed behind.

"Why go back?" one asked the other. "This place may not feel like home, but look at all these crystals." "You're right," said the other, "we can stay here and eat this tasty treasure every day, forever." So the two ants ate crystal after crystal until they were too full to move, and fell asleep.

Daylight came. The sleeping ants were unaware of changes taking place in their new found home. A giant silver scoop hovered above them, then plunged deep into the crystals. It shoveled up both ants and crystals and carried them high into the air.

The ants were wide awake when the scoop turned, dropping them from a frightening height. They tumbled through space in a shower of crystals and fell into a boiling brown lake.

Then the giant scoop stirred violently back and forth. Crushing waves fell over the ants. They paddled hard to keep their tiny heads above water. But the scoop kept spinning the hot brown liquid.

Around and around it went, creating a whirlpool that sucked the ants deeper and deeper. They both held their breath and finally bobbed to the surface, gasping for air and spitting mouthfuls of the terrible, bitter water.

Then the lake tilted and began to empty into a cave. The ants could hear the rushing water and felt themselves pulled toward the pitch black hole. Suddenly the cave disappeared and the lake became calm. The ants swam to the shore and found that the lake had steep sides.

They hurried down the walls that held back the lake. The frightened insects looked for a place to hide, worried that the giant scoop might shovel them up again. Close by they found a huge round disk with holes that could neatly hide them.

But as soon as they climbed inside, their hiding place was lifted, tilted, and lowered into a dark space. When the ants climbed out of the holes they were surrounded by a strange red glow. It seemed to them that every second the temperature was rising.

It soon became so unbearably hot that they thought they would soon be cooked. But suddenly the disk they were standing on rocketed upward and the two hot ants went flying through the air.

STOP AND THINK

Author's Craft The author tells the story from the ants' point of view. How would the story be different if it were told from a person's point of view?

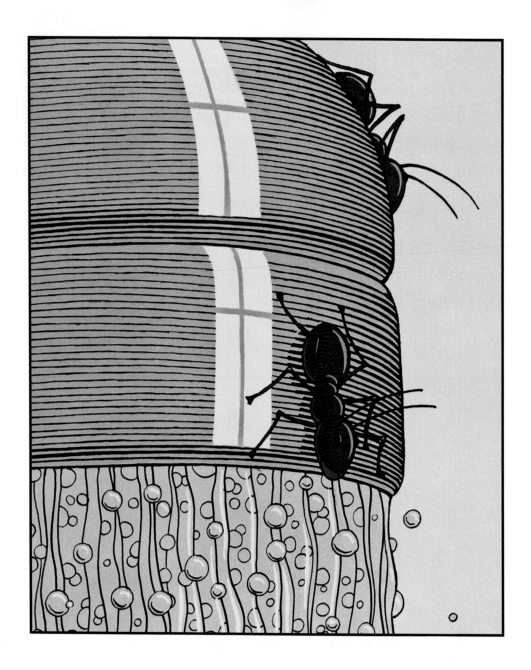

They landed near what seemed to be a fountain—a waterfall pouring from a silver tube. Both ants had a powerful thirst and longed to dip their feverish heads into the fresh water. They quickly climbed along the tube.

As they got closer to the rushing water the ants felt a cool spray. They tightly gripped the shiny surface of the fountain and slowly leaned their heads into the falling stream. But the force of the water was much too strong.

The tiny insects were pulled off the fountain and plunged down into a wet, dark chamber. They landed on half-eaten fruit and other soggy things. Suddenly the air was filled with loud, frightening sounds. The chamber began to spin.

The ants were caught in a whirling storm of shredded food and stinging rain. Then, just as quickly as it had started, the noise and spinning stopped. Bruised and dizzy, the ants climbed out of the chamber.

In daylight once again, they raced through puddles and up a smooth metal wall. In the distance they saw something comforting—two long, narrow holes that reminded them of the warmth and safety of their old underground home. They climbed up into the dark openings.

But there was no safety inside these holes. A strange force passed through the wet ants. They were stunned senseless and blown out of the holes. When they landed the tiny insects were too exhausted to go on. They crawled into a dark corner and fell fast asleep.

Night had returned when the battered ants awoke
to a familiar sound—the footsteps of their fellow insects
returning for more crystals. The two ants slipped quietly to
the end of the line. They climbed the glassy wall and once
again stood amid the treasure. But this time they each chose
a single crystal and followed their friends home.

Standing at the edge of their ant hole, the two ants listened to the joyful sounds that came from below. They knew how grateful their mother queen would be when they gave her their crystals. At that moment, the two ants felt happier than they'd ever felt before. This was their home, this was their family. This was where they were meant to be.

✓ **STOP AND THINK**

Story Structure How might the ending be different if the ants' adventures had been more fun and less scary?

1. Why do the two bad ants stay behind in the new place instead of going home with the other ants?

   ⬭ They are too tired to return home.

   ⬭ The new place feels like home.

   ⬭ The crystals excite them.

   ⬭ They fall asleep right away.

   ELPS 4J

2. ✔ **TARGET SKILL** **Story Structure**

   What happens after the two ants decide not to return to the colony? Use a story map like this. Record details about this part of the story. Write from the ants' point of view. **TEKS** 3.2B

3. ✔ **TARGET STRATEGY** **Monitor/Clarify**

   How can you figure out what is happening to the ants when the author doesn't tell you directly? **TEKS** 3.2C

4. **Oral Language** Use the Retelling Cards to describe story events from the ants' point of view. Have your partner describe these events from an outsider's point of view. Listen carefully to your partner and notice the differences. **TEKS** 3.29A

Retelling Cards

 TEKS 3.2B ask questions/clarify/locate facts/details/use text evidence; **3.2C** establish reading purpose/monitor comprehension; **3.29A** listen/ask questions/make comments; **ELPS** 4J employ inferential skills to demonstrate comprehension

Poems About
Bugs

GENRE

Poetry uses the sound and rhythm of words to show images and express feelings. Discuss how these poets use sound and rhythm in their poems to help you picture what is being described.

TEXT FOCUS

Poets may use **alliteration**, which is repeating the beginning sounds of words, to make the poems more fun to read.

 TEKS 3.6 describe forms of poetry/how they create imagery

Poems About Bugs

The poems you will read next are about bugs. The first poem is a limerick by Edward Lear. A limerick is a short, funny poem with five lines. The first, second, and fifth lines rhyme. So do the third and fourth lines.

A Limerick

There was an Old Man in a tree,
Who was horribly bored by a Bee;
When they said, 'Does it buzz?'
He replied, 'Yes, it does!'
'It's a regular brute of a Bee!'

by Edward Lear

Honeybees live in hives. They enter the hive through narrow openings. Honeybees make a thick, sweet liquid called honey.

Army Ants

Many ants make underground nests, but not army ants. They link their bodies to make a nest above ground. This may seem puzzling, but army ants do not need a real home. They move often, looking for food.

Some ants send out a scout to find food, but not army ants. They move in long columns of more than one-hundred thousand ants! If an animal is unaware of the ants, it is in big trouble. Soon the ants have surrounded it. The army ants bite violently, and the animal becomes their dinner.

The Army Ants

Left
  Right
Left
  Right
We're army ants.
We swarm.
  We fight.
We have no home.
We roam,
We race,
You're lucky if
We miss your place.

by Douglas Florian

193

Upside Down

It's funny how beetles
and creatures like that
can walk upside down
as well as walk flat.

They crawl on a ceiling
and climb on a wall
without any practice
or trouble at all,

While *I* have been trying
for a year (maybe more)
and still I can't stand
with my head on the floor.

by Aileen Fisher

Write a Bug Poem
Write a funny poem about a bug. Try to use the words glassy and soggy in your poem.

Making Connections

Write a Story What adventures would the ants in *Two Bad Ants* have in your kitchen? Write a story in the style of *Two Bad Ants* that tells what would happen. Include details about the setting. Build the story to an exciting finish.

Compare Texts Read the Aesop's tale *The Ant and the Dove*, either in a library book or on the Internet. In a small group, discuss how the lessons the characters learn in this tale and in *Two Bad Ants* are alike and different.

All About Ants On the Internet or in reference books, do research about ants. Find out where they live, what they eat, how they build their homes, and other details about their lives. Prepare a report for your class on your findings.

Grammar

Possessive Nouns and Possessive Pronouns A **possessive noun** shows that a person or an animal owns or has something. Add an apostrophe and -*s* ('*s*) to a singular noun to make it a possessive noun. Add an apostrophe to a plural noun that ends in *s* (*s'*) to make it a possessive noun.

Academic Language

possessive noun

possessive pronoun

Noun	Possessive Noun
mother	mother's face
insect	insect's wings

A pronoun that shows ownership is a **possessive pronoun**.

my   your   her   his   its   our   their

 Write the possessive form of each underlined noun.

❶ queen wish

❸ many chefs hats

❷ several parents toasters

❹ ant antenna

Write each sentence and underline the possessive pronoun.

❺ Beth left her book on the table.

❻ David and Sebastian are riding their new bikes.

196

Ideas When you write, you can make a sentence clearer by adding a possessive noun or possessive pronoun that tells more about the subject. Put the possessive noun or pronoun and any words that go with it right after the subject. Use a comma before and after the words you add.

Less Clear Sentence	Clearer Sentence
Willa watched the ants in her ant farm.	Willa, John's sister, watched the ants in her ant farm.

Less Clear Sentence: The ant farm won first prize in the science fair.

Clearer Sentence: The ant farm, which is mine, won first prize in the science fair.

Connect Grammar to Writing

As you revise your story paragraph, check to see if you can make your sentences clearer. Add possessive nouns and possessive pronouns to tell more about your subjects.

Write to Express

☑ **Ideas** As you read *Two Bad Ants*, were you anxious to find out what would happen next? That feeling is called suspense. Writers create suspense in their stories by giving hints about what *might* happen. See if you can add some suspense to your own **story** paragraphs.

Holly wrote a scene about a brave mouse. Later, she added some details that created more suspense.

Writing Traits Checklist

☑ **Ideas**
Did I add suspense to my story?

☑ **Organization**
Do the characters face problems they have to solve?

☑ **Word Choice**
Did I use vivid words?

☑ **Voice**
Did I include dialogue?

☑ **Sentence Fluency**
Did I use both simple and compound sentences?

☑ **Conventions**
Did I edit for correct grammar?

Revised Draft

"Oh what should I do? " squeaked Emily Mouse. It had poured, and the street was a river. Emily was afraid of water, ∧and couldn't swim but she had to get across. Clara was on the other side. ,Emily's baby, caught in a trap

Soon Emily saw a ∧rusty old tuna can floating toward her. She found a flat little stick, jumped into the can, and began paddling. Emily was too busy to feel her tail and feet getting soaked.

198

The Bravest Mouse

by Holly Becker

"Oh what should I do?" squeaked Emily Mouse. It had poured, and the street was a river. Emily was afraid of water and couldn't swim, but she had to get across. Clara, Emily's baby, was on the other side caught in a trap. Soon Emily saw a rusty old tuna can floating toward her. She found a flat little stick, jumped into the can, and began paddling. Emily was too busy to feel her tail and feet getting soaked. Suddenly, the leaky can sank. Emily's paddle floated away. She began kicking and paddling with her feet. "Hey, I'm swimming!" she thought. "Hang on, Clara. Here I come!"

> I added details that helped build suspense. I also added nouns to a sentence to tell more about the subject.

Reading as a Writer

Which details add suspense to Holly's story? Where can you add suspense in your own story?

migrate

survival

plenty

frightening

accidents

solid

chilly

landscape

thunderous

dramatic

Vocabulary   Context
Reader   Cards

 ELPS **1D** speak using learning
strategies

Vocabulary in Context

1 migrate
These butterflies fly far away when they migrate, or move from place to place.

2 survival
This bluebird flies south for the winter for its survival, or to stay alive.

3 plenty
Some animals don't migrate in winter if they have saved plenty of food.

4 frightening
It is frightening, or scary, for penguins when leopard seals come nearby.

- **Study each Context Card.**
- **Use two Vocabulary words to tell about an experience you had.**

5 accidents

When moose cross busy roads to find food, accidents can happen.

6 solid

It is very hard for animals to find food under snow and solid ice.

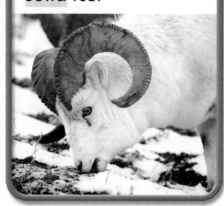

7 chilly

Polar bears have thick fur to keep them warm in cold, chilly weather.

8 landscape

The landscape changes in spring. Grass turns green, and flowers bloom.

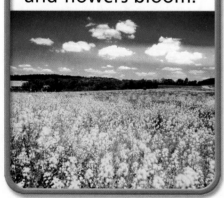

9 thunderous

A herd of caribou makes a very loud, thunderous sound as it runs.

10 dramatic

Salmon swimming upstream to lay eggs is a dramatic, or exciting, sight.

Background

✓ TARGET VOCABULARY   **Migration** Every year, animals migrate. Survival often depends on finding new ways to get enough food, water, or shelter. There may be plenty to eat or drink in one spot during summer but none in the chilly winter. Rivers can freeze into solid ice. As a result, animals must migrate in order to survive.

Sometimes thousands of animals migrate together. This can be a frightening and dramatic sight. They may make a thunderous noise as they cross the landscape. Both animals and people must be careful to avoid accidents!

This map shows the major routes some birds follow when they migrate across North America to warmer southern climates. How many different major routes do you see?

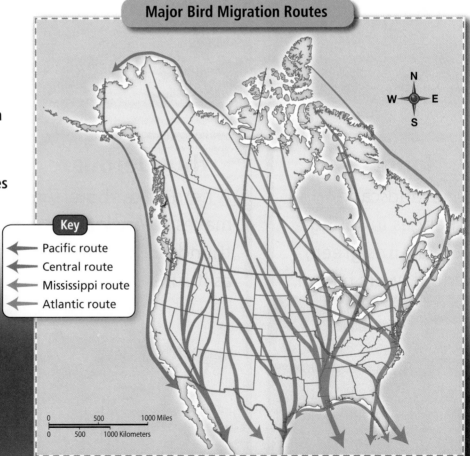

Major Bird Migration Routes

Key
← Pacific route
← Central route
← Mississippi route
← Atlantic route

0   500   1000 Miles
0   500   1000 Kilometers

Comprehension

✔ **TARGET SKILL** **Compare and Contrast**

Find out how a locust's migration compares to that of a gray whale. What is the same, and what is different about these experiences? Use a Venn diagram like this one to compare details about how locusts and whales migrate.

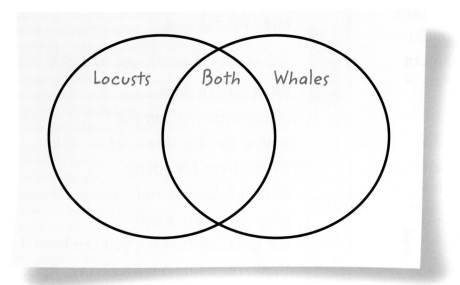

Locusts   Both   Whales

✔ **TARGET STRATEGY** **Visualize**

Use the information in your Venn diagram to help you visualize, or picture, details about whales and locusts. How do they look, sound, and act as they migrate?

Main Selection

TARGET VOCABULARY

migrate	solid
survival	chilly
plenty	landscape
frightening	thunderous
accidents	dramatic

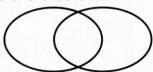

Compare and Contrast

Tell how details or ideas are alike and different.

TARGET STRATEGY

Visualize As you read, use selection details to picture what is happening.

GENRE

Informational text gives factual information about a topic. Use what you know about genre to set a purpose for reading.

 TEKS 3.2C establish reading purpose/ monitor comprehension;

MEET THE AUTHOR

Cynthia Rylant

What advice does an award-winning, famous author like Cynthia Rylant have for young writers? Go out and play. "Playing is still the greatest training you can have, I think, for being a writer," says Rylant. "It helps you love life, it helps you relax, and it helps you cook up interesting stuff in your head." She is the author of *The Blue Hill Meadows* and many other books.

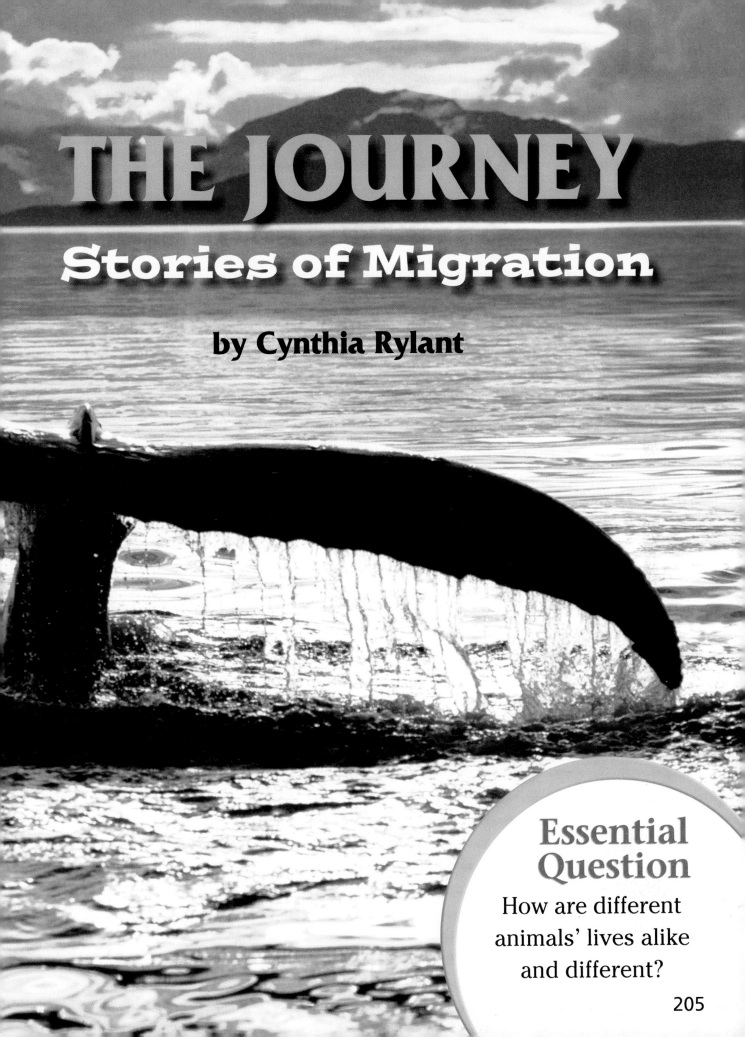

THE JOURNEY
Stories of Migration

by Cynthia Rylant

**Essential
Question**

How are different
animals' lives alike
and different?

Introduction

Most creatures live out their lives in the places where they are born. The tiny mouse runs in the fields where his mother ran. The gray squirrel lives in the same tall trees all her life. The cow stays on the farm.

But there are some creatures who do not stay where they are born, who cannot stay. These are the creatures who migrate. Their lives will be spent moving from one place to another. Some will migrate to survive. Some will migrate to create new life. All will be remarkable.

Here are the stories of two of these remarkable travelers—so different from each other but so alike in one profound way: Each must *move*.

The Locusts

There are few migrations as dramatic and frightening as when the desert locusts are moving across Africa. These insects are actually young grasshoppers, and grasshoppers usually do not travel.

But sometimes too many grasshopper eggs are laid in one small area, and when the grasshoppers are born, there isn't enough food. The grasshoppers now have only one choice for survival: to migrate in search of vegetation.

And so these grasshoppers will begin changing. Their bodies will turn from light green to dark yellow or red. Their antennae will grow short rather than long. And when they rise up to fly together by the *billions*, they will be grasshoppers no more. They will be locusts.

A cloud of desert locusts in the sky is an unbelievable sight. There are so many locusts that they block out the sun. It seems like night. And in the sudden darkness there is a terrible thunderous noise. It is the noise of a billion wings.

STOP AND THINK

Visualize What words and phrases help you visualize how it looks and sounds when the locusts fly away together?

What happens next is even more incredible. When the locusts fly to the ground, they will eat every plant, every blade of grass, every leaf and bush and piece of vegetation as far as the eye can see. Within minutes they will fly off again, leaving behind them a totally devastated landscape.

And though locusts do not willfully hurt people—they want only to eat gardens, trees, bushes, grass—people may die because of the locusts. Because the gardens are empty of food, people may die of starvation.

Desert locusts can also cause accidents. Locusts fly very high—as high as two miles up in the sky—and this can make difficult flying for planes that have to move through the locust cloud. The swarms can also interfere with trains. And millions of crushed locusts on a highway will make cars slip and slide.

There are many stories in history about the terrible devastation of locust plagues. It is written that in ancient times, one locust swarm covered 2,000 square miles.

The swarms today are not nearly as large as that. But they can still be quite big, often as much as one hundred square miles. Imagine so many insects in the sky!

locust eggs

As the locusts migrate in search of food, they ride the winds from one area of rainfall to the next. (There is always more food where it rains.) They travel on sunny mornings and stop in late afternoon to roost for the night.

When they reach a rainy area, they mate and die. Then their eggs will hatch and a new swarm of locusts begins moving. This will happen again and again until one day a swarm will return to the same place where the very first locusts began.

And if the eggs laid are not too many, and if there is plenty of food when the new eggs hatch, there will be no locust swarms for a while. Only pale green grasshoppers moving quietly about.

But someday too many eggs may be laid, and the newly hatched grasshoppers will be much too hungry. These grasshoppers will begin to look a little different and act a little different.

Then they will rise up together by the billions—as desert locusts—and they will fly.

The Whales

Many mammals migrate, but no mammal migrates as far as the big gray whale. It travels 6,000 miles, then back again—and most of its traveling is done on an empty stomach!

Gray whales love the cold waters near the North Pole because the waters are full of the food they love to eat. The whales live on tiny ocean shrimp and worms, and the Arctic waters are full of these in summer. The whales eat and eat and eat, straining the tiny food through strips of baleen in their mouths. (Instead of teeth, the grays have baleen—long strips of a hard material similar to fingernails.)

The gray whales swim and eat mostly alone through the summer. But in the fall, they will begin to look for some traveling companions, because the whales know one thing for certain: that they must migrate. In winter, the Arctic seas are going to be filled with solid ice. And the whales will die if they stay.

The first gray whales to leave the Arctic are the pregnant females. These expectant mothers want to have plenty of time to reach the warm waters of California and Mexico before they give birth. No mother wants to have a baby in icy water!

STOP AND THINK

Author's Craft How does the author make sure readers understand what baleen are and how they work?

The other whales will follow, and in small groups they will all travel down the Pacific coast. Once they leave the Arctic, the whales won't find much food again, and it may be as long as *eight months* before they eat.

But the whales have stored a lot of fat in their bodies, called blubber, and this will keep them alive.

As they travel, the whales often swim near shore, and people along the way are thrilled. They wave to the whales from rocky cliffs and travel out in boats to say hello to them.

When finally the gray whales reach the warm tropical waters in January, the pregnant females will give birth. And the other whales will mate.

With new calves among them, all of the whales will enjoy life in the peaceful lagoons for a while. Then in March, they will be ready to head back to the Arctic for the summer. They haven't forgotten how they love to eat there!

This time the males will leave first, and the females and calves will stay behind for another several weeks. The calves will have more time to grow and get stronger for the long journey.

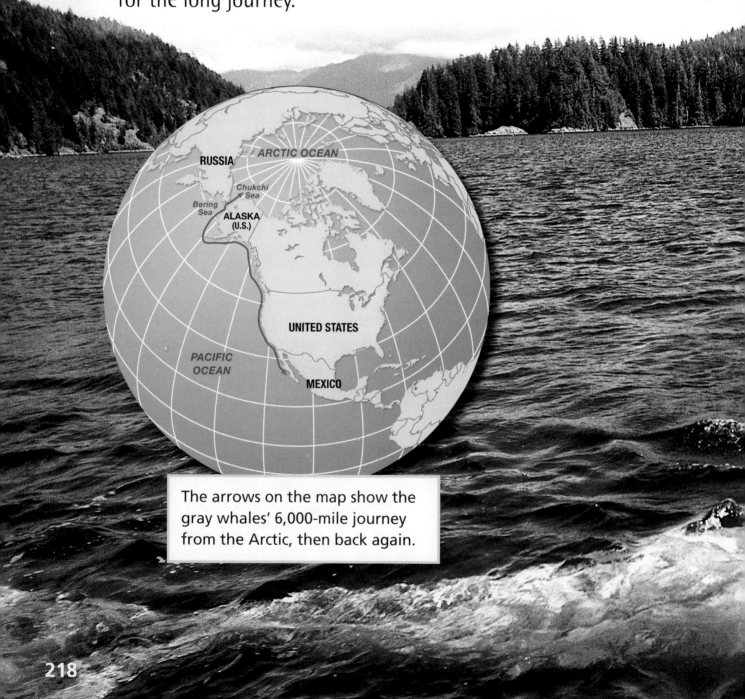

The arrows on the map show the gray whales' 6,000-mile journey from the Arctic, then back again.

Finally, all of the whales will travel, up past Oregon, past Washington, through the waters of Alaska and Asia, up near the North Pole. How do the whales find these Arctic waters? No one is sure. The whales might follow the shape of the ocean beds. They might sense the earth's magnetic field, like living compasses. They may use echolocation—sending out sounds which bounce back and describe what is all around.

But somehow the whales will travel that long 6,000-mile journey north, and they will find the same chilly waters they left behind. When they arrive in the Arctic, they will separate and enjoy a summer of fine ocean eating.

✔ STOP AND THINK

Compare and Contrast What is the same about the two trips whales make? What is different?

But just before the Arctic winter arrives, before the ice, something will tell the whales to find each other again. To find some company for another long, long swim.

Your Turn

1. Which words from page 206 help the reader know what migrate means?

   ⬭ *live out their lives*

   ⬭ *do not stay where they are born*

   ⬭ *will be remarkable*

   ⬭ *so different from each other*

2. ✔ **TARGET SKILL** **Compare and Contrast**

   Use a Venn diagram like this to show how grasshoppers and locusts are the same and how they are different. **TEKS** 3.2B

   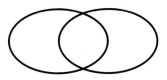

3. ✔ **TARGET STRATEGY** **Visualize**

   Picture a park in your town. Describe what it looks like now and what it would look like after a swarm of locusts has landed there. Use what you read to imagine the scene.

4. **Oral Language** Use the Retelling Cards to explain to a partner how and why locusts and whales migrate. Look at your partner as you speak. **TEKS** 3.30; **ELPS** 4G

   Retelling Cards

 TEKS **3.2B** ask questions/clarify/locate facts/details/use text evidence; **3.30** speak coherently/effectively about topics; **ELPS** **4G** demonstrate comprehension through shared reading/retelling/responding/note-taking

The Grasshopper and the Ant

an **Aesop's fable** adapted by **Margaretha Rabe**

Grasshopper loved to sing and play his fiddle. He played quiet songs and thunderous tunes. Sometimes Grasshopper played frightening music. Then he would hop around in a dramatic way. That's when he caused accidents.

One time Grasshopper jumped into a pile of grain that Ant had spent all day collecting. The grain scattered across the landscape.

"You should be more careful, Grasshopper," scolded Ant. "I worked hard to gather that grain. Now I have to pile it up again."

"I'm sorry," said Grasshopper. "Why not take a break? It's a beautiful, sunny day. You'll have plenty of days to gather food."

"You may think so, Grasshopper, but winter will soon be here. Then the ground will be frozen solid," said Ant. "Now is the time to gather food and plan for survival. You should take a break from playing and do some work."

Grasshopper said, "I'll migrate to someplace warm if it gets too chilly. That way, I can keep on playing and singing. But for now I'll play any song you like to make your work easier to do."

Weeks later, fat flakes of snow began to drift from the sky. Grasshopper shivered. It was so cold that he could hardly hold his fiddle. Grasshopper looked for food, but the ground had turned into a blanket of white snow.

"What will I do now? I can't find food, and it's too cold for me to go far. Maybe Ant will help me," thought Grasshopper.

Grasshopper trudged through the snow and knocked on Ant's door. "Will you give me food if I sing and play for you?" asked Grasshopper.

Ant said, "Yes I will. I worked hard the rest of the year, so now I have time to relax and have fun."

Moral: There are times to work and times to play.

Making Connections

Text to Self
TEKS 3.19; ELPS 5G

Grasshopper or Ant? In *Grasshopper and the Ant*, Grasshopper likes to play, and Ant is always working. Are you more like Grasshopper or Ant? Or are you a little bit like both? Write a paragraph explaining your answer and giving examples.

Text to Text
TEKS 3.30, RC-3(F); ELPS 2I

Respond to Questions Choose an animal from this week's reading to interview. Work with a partner. One of you should role-play the animal. The other should ask and answer questions and respond to requests about what the animal needs to prepare for winter. Make sure you understand your partner's answers.

Text to World
ELPS 5G

Connect to Science You read that locusts and whales migrate. Use the library or Internet to find out about another animal that migrates. Make a poster or other display to show what you learned.

 TEKS **3.19** write about personal experiences; **3.30** speak coherently/effectively about topics; **RC-3(F)** make connections between texts; **ELPS** **2I** demonstrate listening comprehension of spoken English; **5G** narrate/describe/explain in writing

Grammar

Using Proper Nouns There are many kinds of **proper nouns**. Names for days, months, holidays, and titles of people are proper nouns. Always begin a proper noun with a capital letter. Include a comma after the number in dates.

Academic Language

proper noun

Thursday	March
Saturday	December
July 24, 2012	Labor Day
August 10, 1949	Memorial Day
Mrs. Emma J. Lopez	Officer Wilson
Mr. Brian Chang	Governor Peterson

 Try This! **Write each sentence correctly. Remember to punctuate the date correctly.**

❶ School will be closed next monday.

❷ It is columbus day.

❸ My teacher, mr. wade, told us about something to do on the day off.

❹ We might see the locust migration on october 8 2011.

❺ doctor ortez will give a talk at the hospital.

226

Ideas In your writing, you can make a sentence clearer by adding words that tell when. You can also include a proper noun for days, months, or holidays.

Less Clear Sentence	Clearer Sentence
We saw a whale swimming off the coast last winter.	We saw a whale swimming off the coast last winter on New Year's Day.

Grammar in Writing

As you revise your descriptive paragraph, try to add words that tell when. Be sure to use capital letters, commas, and periods correctly.

Write to Express

☑ **Word Choice** In *The Journey: Stories of Migration*, you read that a billion locusts' wings sound like thunder. *Like thunder* is a simile, which is a phrase that uses *like* or *as* to compare two things.

Ethan wrote a **description** of a canary. Later, he added similes to help his readers see, hear, and feel the bird.

Writing Traits Checklist

☑ **Ideas**
Did I use details for at least three of the five senses?

☑ **Organization**
Did I tell my details in a clear order?

☑ **Word Choice**
Did I use similes?

☑ **Voice**
Do my feelings come through?

☑ **Sentence Fluency**
Did I use phrases that tell where and when?

☑ **Conventions**
Did I edit my work for spelling, grammar, and punctuation?

Revised Draft

Zack was a little canary. He

belonged to a boy named Mike.
Zack was ̲b̲r̲i̲g̲h̲t̲ ̲y̲e̲l̲l̲o̲w̲. ^as yellow as the sun. He had

^like tiny glass beads
black eyes, and his beak was small

and pointed. Under his beak, his

^like kitten fur
feathers were soft and puffy, but

his wings and tail were smooth. He

^as skinny as toothpicks
hopped around on ̲s̲k̲i̲n̲n̲y̲ legs.

^Every morning,
Zack had a great voice. He sang

loudly and cheerfully.

228

Zack

by Ethan Washington

Zack was a little canary. He belonged to a boy named Mike. Zack was as yellow as the sun. He had black eyes like tiny glass beads, and his beak was small and pointed. Under his beak, his feathers were soft and puffy like kitten fur, but his wings and tail were smooth. He hopped around on legs as skinny as toothpicks. Zack had a great voice. Every morning, he sang loudly and cheerfully. He sounded like a person whistling. Sometimes he liked to perch on Mike's shoulder when he sang. Zack was a happy, friendly bird.

> I added similes to help readers picture Zack. I also added a phrase that tells when.

Reading as a Writer

What similes did Ethan use to describe Zack? Where can you add similes in your paper?

229

Vocabulary in Context

The Journey of OLIVER K. WOODMAN

Moving the U.S. Mail

✔ **TARGET VOCABULARY**

sincere

managed

loaded

loveliest

conversations

inspired

reunion

currently

pleasure

terror

Vocabulary Reader

Context Cards

Route 66

TEKS 3.4E alphabetize to third letter/ use dictionary/glossary

230

1 sincere

This President had sincere hopes. He truly wanted to change unfair laws.

2 managed

Artists managed to carve this special monument. It was not easy!

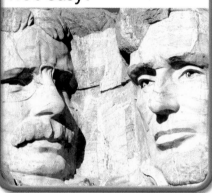

3 loaded

Before sailing, people loaded onto this swan boat. They piled on.

4 loveliest

Oregon's Crater Lake is one of the loveliest national parks. It is beautiful.

- Study each Context Card.
- Place the Vocabulary words in alphabetical order.

5 conversations

Conversations in a museum must be quiet. People should speak in whispers.

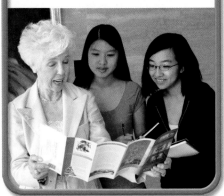

6 inspired

This statue has inspired people. It makes them believe in freedom.

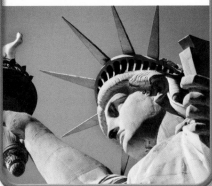

7 reunion

This family went camping for their yearly reunion, or gathering.

8 currently

Currently, this fort is a museum. Soldiers no longer live here.

9 pleasure

People get pleasure, or enjoyment, from riding this old merry-go-round.

10 terror

When people look down at the Grand Canyon they may feel terror, or fear.

Background

✔ TARGET VOCABULARY **Traveling Now and Then** Are you ever inspired to travel? Currently, we travel easily by planes, trains, or cars. We can enjoy snacks and conversations flying 30,000 feet high! Long ago, people managed to travel, but it was difficult and often dangerous. Some travelers felt terror as they loaded onto horse-drawn wagons, camels, or creaky ships.

Travel today is fun and teaches us many new things. Loveliest of all, though, may be the sincere pleasure of coming home to a reunion with loved ones.

Travel Today	Travel Long Ago
Airplanes	Walking or horseback riding
Trains	Horse-drawn wagons
Cars and buses	Camels in caravan, or long line
Steam or gas-powered boat	Open boat or wind-powered ship
Interstate highways	Rough dirt roads or trails

People still use camels to travel, just as they did thousands of years ago!

TEKS **3.16B** explain influence of media design techniques; **3.8A** sequence/summarize main events/influence on future events; **ELPS 4K** employ analytical skills to demonstrate comprehension

Comprehension

✓ **TARGET SKILL** **Sequence of Events**

As you read *The Journey of Oliver K. Woodman*, notice the sequence, or order, in which events take place. Use dates, times of day, and signal words to help you put the events in sequence on a chart like this one.

Event

↓

Event

↓

Event

✓ **TARGET STRATEGY** **Analyze/Evaluate**

The author uses letters to tell this story. What do you think of her choice to tell the story that way? Does it make story events easier or more difficult to follow? Does it make reading the story more or less enjoyable?

The Journey of OLIVER K. WOODMAN

✔ **TARGET VOCABULARY**

sincere	inspired
managed	reunion
loaded	currently
loveliest	pleasure
conversations	terror

✔ **TARGET SKILL**

Sequence of Events
Tell the time order in which
events happen.

Analyze/Evaluate Think
about what you read. Then
form an opinion about it.

GENRE
A **fantasy** is a story that
could not happen in real life.
As you read, ask yourself
these questions: *Which
details are realistic? Which
are make believe?*

TEKS **3.2B** ask questions/clarify/locate
facts/details/use text evidence

MEET THE AUTHOR
Darcy Pattison
Oliver K. Woodman, the
character Darcy Pattison
created, has become so
popular that students at schools in
New York, Indiana, and other states
have their own wooden models of him.
Whenever they travel, they take Oliver
with them and bring back photos and
journal entries from his journey.

MEET THE ILLUSTRATOR
Joe Cepeda
Joe Cepeda does
woodworking as a
hobby, so when he was
illustrating this story he drew Oliver K.
Woodman as if he were really going
to build the character out of wood.
Author Darcy Pattison loves how
Cepeda's art turned out. "Oliver has
no mouth, yet you would swear that
he's smiling at us," she says.

THE JOURNEY OF OLIVER K. WOODMAN

written by
Darcy Pattison

illustrated by
Joe Cepeda

Essential Question

What happens
if you tell story
events out of order?

May 10
Redcrest, CA

Dear Uncle Ray,
   Please come to visit us this summer.
We will go camping. We can swim and
catch fish.
   You are my favorite uncle. Please say
you will come!

   Love,
   Tameka
   XOXOXO

May 17
Rock Hill, SC

Dear Tameka,

I'd love to come to California, but I can't.
I will be building kitchen cabinets for some new
apartments all summer.

But maybe my friend Oliver will come to visit!

Love,
Uncle Ray

 STOP AND THINK

Sequence of Events Who wrote
the first letter, Uncle Ray or Tameka?
How can you figure this out?

TEKS 3.2B **ELPS** 4K

Dear Traveler,

I am going to see Tameka Schwartz, 370 Park Avenue, Redcrest, California, 95569. Please give me a ride and help me get there. If you don't mind, drop a note to my friend Raymond Johnson, 111 Stony Lane, Rock Hill, South Carolina, 29730. He wants to keep up with my travels.

Thanks,
Oliver K. Woodman

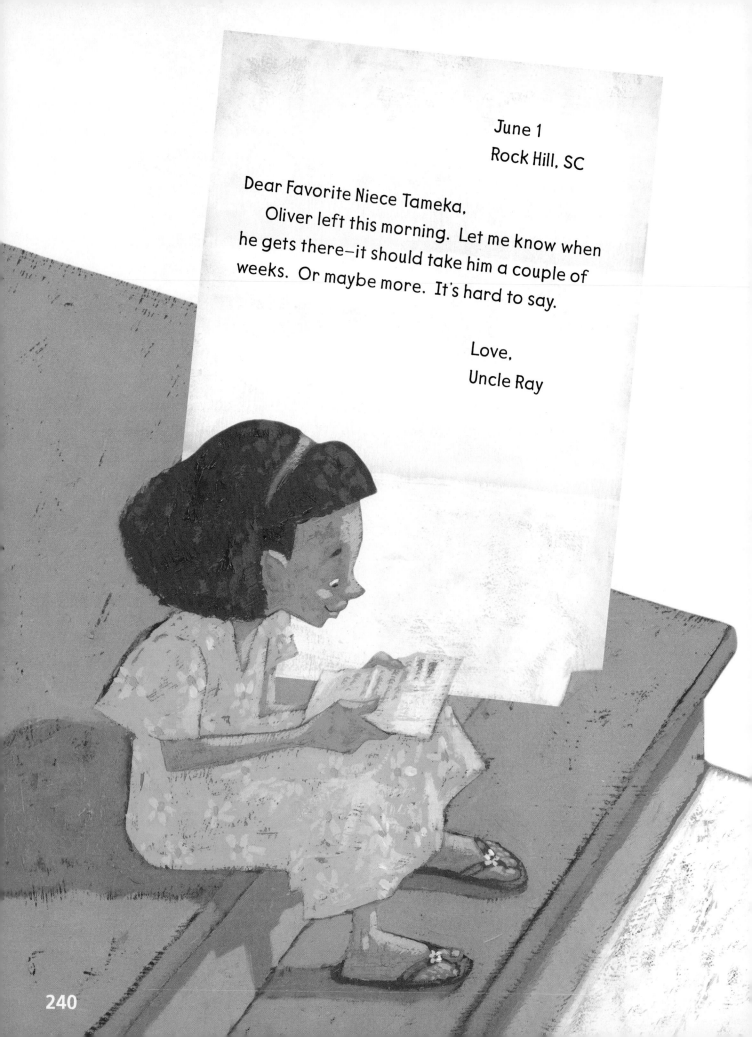

June 1
Rock Hill, SC

Dear Favorite Niece Tameka,
Oliver left this morning. Let me know when
he gets there—it should take him a couple of
weeks. Or maybe more. It's hard to say.

Love,
Uncle Ray

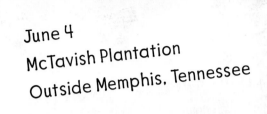

June 4
McTavish Plantation
Outside Memphis, Tennessee

Dear Ray:
    For two days, Oliver rode in the back of my truck and kept Bert, my Brahman bull, company. I delivered Bert to his new home and he's settling in, but he'll miss the late-night conversations and singing with Oliver.
    I left Oliver east of the Mississippi River, just outside Memphis, and hurried home to my beloved Amelia.

        Yours truly,
        Jackson McTavish

June 8
Forrest City, AR

Hi! Mr. OK is OK. Quinn and Sherry
went to a basketball game at The Pyramid in
Memphis, Tennessee, last weekend and
brought Mr. OK back. He hung out with us for
a couple of days, and all the girls liked him
better than Quinn. So when Quinn's cousin's
boyfriend's aunt was leaving to visit her sick
grandfather in Fort Smith, Arkansas, the
guys loaded Mr. OK into the aunt's station
wagon and sent him on his way. We didn't
even get to say good-bye!

Raymond Johnson
111 Stony Lane
Rock Hill, SC 29730

Cherry (Sherry's sister),
for the Gang

P.S. If you see Mr. OK again, tell him
we all said good-bye.

STOP AND THINK

Author's Craft How does
Cherry's letter sound different
from Jackson's letter on
page 241? Which details
make it sound this way?

June 11
Albuquerque, NM

Hey, Ray—
    I drive a moving van for
Southeast Moving Company. I picked
up Oliver at the Arkansas border,
then drove west to Oklahoma City,
Oklahoma, south to Dallas, Texas,
northwest to Amarillo, Texas, east to
Panhandle, Texas, then west again to
Albuquerque, New Mexico.
    He's an easy fella to travel with.
He never needs bathroom stops. He
doesn't care where we eat. And he
stays awake with me all night. I'm
sorry to see him go, but this week the
company is sending me east, to
Wauchula, Florida.
                Trucking along—
                Bobbi Jo

Raymond Johnson
111 Stony Lane
Rock Hill, SC 29730

June 28
Rock Hill, SC

Dear Tameka,
I've had no word from Oliver in seventeen days.
I'm starting to worry. What if he is lost?
Please call me if he turns up at your house.

Love,
Uncle Ray

July 1
Redcrest, CA

Dear Uncle Ray,

No word from Oliver. Are you sure he's really coming?

I still wish we could see you. I asked Mama if we could come visit, but she said it costs too much. Daddy says he can't take off work that long. Ever since I asked, Mama keeps looking at family photo albums. When she sees your pictures, she says, "My baby brother!"

Love,
Tameka
XOXOXOX

July 4
Salt Lake City, UT

Dear Raymond Johnson:
My grandfather found Mr. Woodman in the middle of the reservation in New Mexico. Poor fella—a mouse was building a nest in his backpack. We don't know how he ended up way out there, and he's not telling.
Grandpa brought him to Utah to join me in the Fourth of July parade. I got so tired of smiling and waving at the crowds, but Mr. Woodman's brave smile inspired me.
I just sent Mr. Woodman off with three sisters. They looked like such nice old ladies, so I know they'll take good care of him.

With all my love—
Melissa Tso, Miss Utah

P.S. I've enclosed an autographed picture.

July 27
en route to San Francisco, CA

Dear Mr. Johnson:

My sisters and I had the distinct pleasure of entertaining Mr. Oliver K. Woodman for the past 23 days.

You see, we've lived in Kokomo, Indiana, all our lives. Until now, we'd never been west of the Mississippi River. Our dear papa died in January and left us an inheritance. We decided to use the money to tour the West this year.

While in Salt Lake City, we saw Mr. Oliver in a parade, and after talking it over, we voted to give him a ride. We stopped at a rodeo in Eureka, Nevada, where Mr. Oliver

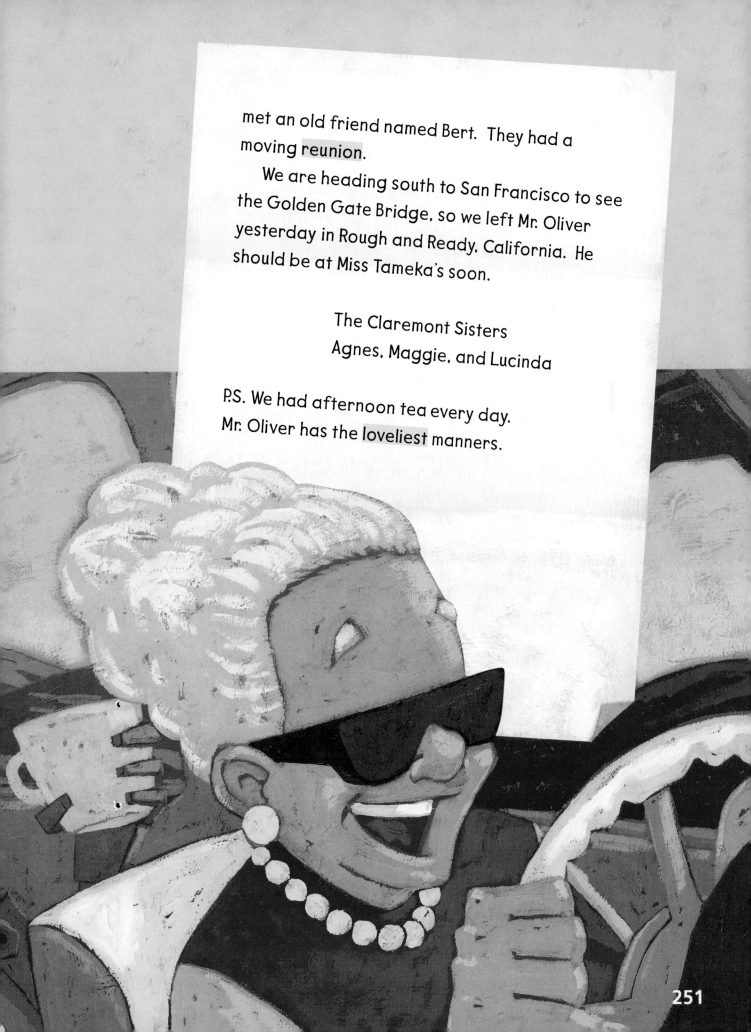

met an old friend named Bert. They had a moving reunion.

We are heading south to San Francisco to see the Golden Gate Bridge, so we left Mr. Oliver yesterday in Rough and Ready, California. He should be at Miss Tameka's soon.

The Claremont Sisters
Agnes, Maggie, and Lucinda

P.S. We had afternoon tea every day. Mr. Oliver has the loveliest manners.

July 28
To: Raymond Johnson
Re: Mr. Oliver K. Woodman

Our family, currently on vacation, picked up the above-named person in what I thought was a misguided goodwill gesture. Little did I know how lucky that gesture would be.

Last night, we pitched tents in the Redwood forest. I woke at 3:00 A.M. to screams of terror. Bears! Your friend managed to frighten them away. He saved our lives.

With the deepest and most sincere gratitude, we intend to deliver him to the doorstep of Tameka Schwartz within the next two days.

Gratefully yours,
Bernard Grape,
Attorney-at-Law

Raymond Johnson
111 Stony Lane
Rock Hill, SC
29730

✔ STOP AND THINK
Analyze/Evaluate Why do you think the author decided to tell the story with letters?

August 1
Redcrest, CA

Dear Uncle Ray,

Guess who came to dinner? Oliver!
He is so much fun! We are camping in the backyard tonight. I hear he's not scared of anything, so I'm glad he'll be there. Tomorrow, at the river, I'll let him hold my fishing pole while I swim.

Guess what else? Daddy and Mama talked it over. We're coming to your house next month, and we'll bring Oliver home. Isn't it wonderful?

Love,
Tameka
XOXOXOX

P.S. Knock, knock. Who's there? Olive. Olive who? Olive both you and Oliver!

Oliver's Journey

ROCK HILL CITY NEWS
SEPTEMBER 15

TICKER-TAPE PARADE FOR HOMETOWN BOY

by Demetrius Dickson

Oliver K. Woodman will return home today amid national acclaim for his cross-country journey. Woodman began his trip on June 1, in Rock Hill, South Carolina, and arrived in Redcrest, California, on August 1.

The Rock Hill City Council announced that a ticker-tape parade to honor Woodman will be held today at 10:00 A.M., starting at the corner of Main Street and Cherry Road and proceeding down Cherry Road to Cherry Park.

Raymond Johnson and Tameka Schwartz, friends of Mr. Woodman, will host a picnic in his honor at Cherry Park at noon. At 1:00 P.M., Mr. Woodman will show postcards and mementos from his trip. The public is invited.

Your Turn

1. For what reason does Oliver K. Woodman set off on a trip to see Tameka?

   ⬭ Uncle Ray is too busy to write letters to Tameka.

   ⬭ Oliver wants to have an adventure.

   ⬭ Oliver and Tameka are best friends.

   ⬭ Uncle Ray cannot visit Tameka during the summer.

2. ✔ **TARGET SKILL** **Sequence of Events**

   Tameka wrote to Uncle Ray, asking him to visit. Use a chart like the one below to show events between then and when Uncle Ray's letter got to Tameka on June 1. **TEKS** 3.8A

3. ✔ **TARGET STRATEGY** **Analyze/Evaluate**

   What does the information in the chart above tell you about Uncle Ray? **TEKS** 3.2B

4. **Oral Language** Work with a partner. Use the Retelling Cards to describe the people Oliver met. Don't talk too fast or too slowly. **TEKS** 3.30

   Retelling Cards

 TEKS **3.2B** ask questions/clarify/locate facts/details/use text evidence; **3.8A** sequence/summarize main events/influence on future events; **3.30** speak coherently/effectively about topics

Connect to
Social Studies

✓ TARGET VOCABULARY

sincere	inspired
managed	reunion
loaded	currently
loveliest	pleasure
conversations	terror

GENRE

Informational text gives factual information about a topic. This is an online encyclopedia.

TEXT FOCUS

A **timeline** is a line that shows the order in which events happened. Discuss the timeline shown here. Try to figure out the year each form of transportation was used by the United States Postal Service.

TEKS **3.13D** use text features to locate information/make and verify predictions; **3.15B** locate/use graphic features of text; **ELPS** **3J** respond orally to information in media; **4K** employ analytical skills to demonstrate comprehension

Moving the U.S. Mail

The United States Postal Service

The United States Postal Service has changed over the years. In colonial times, all kinds of people helped deliver mail. Sometimes letters managed to get through. Sometimes they didn't.

Delivery Times
New York to San Francisco

1800

Pony Express 13–14 days by train to Missouri, then on horseback

Getting mail brings pleasure to many, but it has never been easy to deliver. Today the Postal Service makes a sincere effort to deliver all mail. Currently it delivers hundreds of millions of messages daily.

Transportation Changes

Having conversations by mail has gotten much faster. Why is this? Transportation has improved. Long ago, people carried mail on foot, horseback, and stagecoaches. Today's mail is loaded onto trucks and planes.

In 1775 Benjamin Franklin became the first Postmaster General.

1900   **2000**

Transcontinental Railroad 7 days

Airplane 6–7 hours

Golden Moments of Mail History

Gold was discovered in California in 1848. People rushed west. The California Gold Rush inspired faster mail delivery. It would be a long time until they could have a reunion with their families, so gold seekers wanted mail from home.

Pony Express riders carried mail to California in 1860 and 1861. Their rides could be full of terror. They faced blizzards and bandits.

By 1869 the Transcontinental Railroad linked railroads in the east with California. The mail moved faster than ever.

A Postmark from the Heart

Each year around February 14, mail from around the world takes a detour. This mail isn't slowed by blizzards or bandits—it's delayed by love! In honor of Valentine's Day, cards are mailed to the small town of Valentine, Texas. They get the town's postmark and go on to their final destination.

Each year, in Valentine, Texas, the school holds a design contest. The city council chooses the loveliest design to be used as that year's postmark.

Aunt Susie
123 Msososo Street
Austin, TX 12307

260

Making Connections

 Text to Self

TEKS 3.20B; ELPS 5G

Write a Letter What would you do with Oliver K. Woodman if he visited you? Write a letter to Uncle Ray about the adventures you would have. Include a date, greeting, and closing. Use friendly, informal language.

 Text to Text

TEKS 3.2B

Compare and Contrast What if Oliver had traveled to California by Pony Express? Would his trip be shorter or longer? How else would it be similar to or different from his travels in *The Journey of Oliver K. Woodman?* Use information from "Moving the U.S. Mail" to help you write a paragraph about Oliver's trip by Pony Express.

 Text to World

TEKS 3.26A(iii); ELPS 4F

Connect to Social Studies Use a road map of the United States to find the places that Oliver K. Woodman visited. Identify the general direction in which he traveled.

 TEKS **3.2B** ask questions/clarify/locate facts/details/use text evidence; **3.20B** write letters tailored to audience/purpose; **3.26A(iii)** collect information from visual sources; **ELPS** **4F** use visual/contextual/peer/teacher support to read/comprehend texts; **5G** narrate/describe/explain in writing

Grammar

Abbreviations An **abbreviation** is a short way to write a word. Most abbreviations begin with a capital letter and end with a period.

Academic Language

abbreviation

Some Common Abbreviations					
Months	February	Feb.	April	Apr.	October	Oct.
	March	Mar.	August	Aug.	December	Dec.
Days	Saturday	Sat.	Monday	Mon.	Wednesday	Wed.
	Sunday	Sun.	Tuesday	Tues.	Thursday	Thurs.
Addresses	Street	St.	Road	Rd.	Avenue	Ave.

 Write the abbreviation for each day, month, or street name below.

1. Saturday

2. December

3. Avenue

4. March 28

5. 325 Elm Road

6. Wednesday, August 6, 1999

7. November 3

8. 932 Swanton Street

Conventions You can use abbreviations for the titles of people in many kinds of writing. Usually, you abbreviate the names of days, months, and kinds of streets only in addresses and lists.

Incorrect	Correct
mon., jan 6 Baseball Card Club meets at mrs Joy Cho's home 222 Allen st	Mon., Jan. 6 Baseball Card Club meets at Mrs. Joy Cho's home 222 Allen St.
wed, feb 11 Stamp Club Dinner at the home of dr Calvin Cook 1740 Parker ave	Wed., Feb. 11 Stamp Club Dinner at the home of Dr. Calvin Cook 1740 Parker Ave.

Connect Grammar to Writing

As you edit your dialogue, check to make sure you have used capital letters, commas, and periods correctly.

TEKS 3.17D edit drafts; **3.18A** write imaginative stories; **3.23D** use correct mechanics; **ELPS 5F** use a variety of sentence types in writing; **5G** narrate/describe/explain in writing

Write to Express

☑ **Voice** In *The Journey of Oliver K. Woodman*, you can tell how Tameka feels when she says in a letter, "You are my favorite uncle. Please say you will come!" As you revise your **dialogue**, be sure your characters speak in a way that shows their feelings.

Ava wrote about two girls who find a cave. When Ava revised her draft, her changes showed the girls' feelings.

Writing Traits Checklist

☑ **Ideas**
Is my dialogue interesting?

☑ **Organization**
Can my readers tell what is happening?

☑ **Word Choice**
Did I use formal or informal words that suit my characters?

☑ **Voice**
Do my characters' feelings show?

☑ **Sentence Fluency**
Did I use different kinds of sentences?

☑ **Conventions**
Did I indent each paragraph?

Revised Draft

Mia and Jade were exploring the woods behind their new house. "Hey, I ~~found something,~~ look at this!" whispered Mia.

"It's a cave! Wow, " said Jade. "Let's go in."

"Are you kidding?"
~~"No, I don't want to."~~

"Why not?"

"There could be bears in there!"

Jade smiled. "Don't be silly. ~~I don't think so.~~"

264

The Cave

by Ava Garcia

Mia and Jade were exploring the woods behind their new house. "Hey, look at this!" whispered Mia.

"Wow, a cave!" said Jade. "Let's go in."

"Are you kidding?"

"Why not?"

"There could be bears in there!"

Jade smiled. "Don't be silly. Mrs. Chen said there are no bears around here."

Mia said, "Well, I have a cold, and Dr. David says damp places are bad for colds."

"You're just scared. I'm going in. I bet there's something fantastic in there."

"Well...okay. Let's go," said Mia.

> I added words that show my characters' feelings. I also made sure to write abbreviations correctly.

Reading as a Writer

Which parts let you really hear how each girl feels? Where can you show your own characters' feelings more clearly?

Lesson 24

✓ TARGET VOCABULARY

voyage

lava

rippled

arrival

guided

twisted

aboard

anchor

spotted

bay

Vocabulary Reader | Context Cards

Sea Lions

ELPS 1D speak using learning strategies

266

Vocabulary in Context

1 voyage
The explorer's voyage, or ocean trip, to Hawaii took more than a year.

2 lava
Hawaii's islands formed from lava, or hot melted rock, from volcanoes.

3 rippled
This lava in Hawaii rippled into tiny black waves as it cooled.

4 arrival
When visitors first come to Hawaii, their arrival is welcomed.

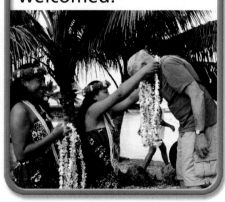

● **Study each Context Card.**

● **Tell a story about two or more pictures, using their Vocabulary words.**

5 guided

This man **guided**, or led, tourists through a park in Hawaii.

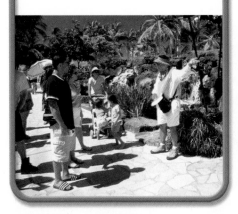

6 twisted

These girls **twisted** wire around flowers to attach them to crowns.

7 aboard

Each racing canoe has six people **aboard**. They are seated in the boat.

8 anchor

A heavy **anchor** holds this boat in place when the boat is stopped.

9 spotted

Whales can be **spotted**, or seen, in the ocean near Hawaii.

10 bay

People can swim, snorkel, or sail in the gentle waters of this **bay**, or inlet.

Background

TARGET VOCABULARY **Seals at Play** When aboard a ship for an ocean voyage, it's fun to look for seals. Seals are playful creatures. They can easily be spotted looking for supper in deep water rippled with fish. They also love splashing around in the shallow water of a harbor or a bay.

   To a seal, the arrival of a new boat means a chance to make new friends. After the boat has been guided into port and the anchor lowered, the seals gather, showing off with tricks. They hope to earn a tasty treat as a reward.

Monk seals in Hawaii like sunbathing on rocks formed from cooled lava. Sadly, they are at risk of dying out. Some monk seals get twisted and tangled in fishing nets.

Comprehension

✓ **TARGET SKILL** **Author's Purpose**

As you read *Dog-of-the-Sea-Waves*, think about the words and ideas the author uses to describe Hawaii. Write these details on a chart like this one. Then use the details to help you figure out the author's purpose, or reason, for writing the story.

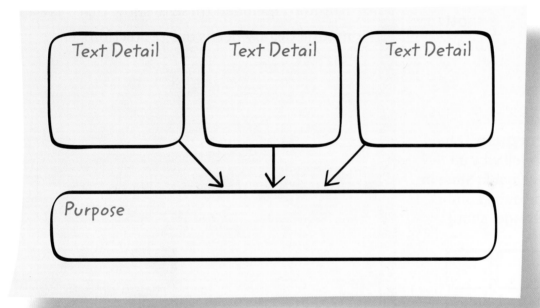

✓ **TARGET STRATEGY** **Question**

As you read, ask yourself, *What does the author want you to learn from the selection?* Details from the story can help you answer the question.

Main Selection

MEET THE AUTHOR AND ILLUSTRATOR

James Rumford

A longtime resident of Hawaii, James Rumford hopes his readers will learn *aloha ʻaina,* or "to cherish these special islands," as much as he does. Scattered throughout the pages of *Dog-of-the-Sea-Waves* are tiny drawings of plants and animals that are found in Hawaii. Many of them are at risk of dying out. Rumford included these to show that Hawaii's natural beauty needs our protection.

✓ TARGET VOCABULARY

voyage	twisted
lava	aboard
rippled	anchor
arrival	spotted
guided	bay

✓ TARGET SKILL

Author's Purpose Use text details to tell why an author writes a book. State in your own words the author's theme, or message, about Hawaii.

✓ TARGET STRATEGY

Question Ask questions before you read, while you read, and after you read.

GENRE

Realistic fiction is a story with events that could happen in real life.

TEKS **3.5A** paraphrase themes/details of tales; **RC-3(D)** make inferences/use textual evidence **ELPS** **4J** employ inferential skills to demonstrate comprehension

Dog-of-the-Sea-Waves

By James Rumford

Essential Question

Why might a writer tell a story about a faraway place?

Five brothers explore the Hawaiian Islands. Manu, the youngest brother, saves the life of an injured seal and the two become friends. When it's time for the brothers to go home, Manu is unsure if he'll ever see his friend again.

O'ahu Tree Snail

In the days when the sun, the moon, and the stars guided birds with seeds in their bellies to these islands, when ocean waves brought driftwood teeming with life, when storms brought frightened birds in the clouds and insects on the wind, the Hawaiian Islands grew green and lush.

The streams and lagoons rippled with fish. And the forests flashed with the feathers of birds and the rainbow wings of insects.

Belted Wrasse

273

The Hawaiian Islands welcomed all life that made the long, long journey to its shores, and some two thousand years ago, they embraced the first people to come.

In those days of first canoes, first footprints, first campfires, there were five brothers who came from their home far to the south to explore these islands. They were Hōkū, who loved the stars, Nāʻale, who loved the sea, ʻŌpua, who loved clouds, Makani, who loved the wind, and Manu, who loved birds.

Kamehameha Butterfly

One night, soon after their arrival, Hōkū said, "See, my brothers, that new star I've discovered? It always points north!"

Everyone except Manu looked up at the sparkling North Star. Everyone except Manu began talking excitedly about all the other new things they had discovered.

"New things!" Manu exclaimed. "I miss the old things. Where are the coconuts, the bananas, the sweet potatoes? And how about the pigs, the chickens, the dogs?"

"We'll go home and bring these things back here with us," said Hōkū.

"We're coming back?" Manu cried. "I don't want to come back. I just want to go home."

But home was a long ocean voyage away, and there was much to do before they could leave—food and water to gather and sails to repair. So no one spoke.

The next day, as the brothers were exploring a lagoon, Manu spotted an animal lying at the water's edge.

"It's a dog, my brothers! A dog!"

At last! Something familiar in this strange land.

But when they got close, they saw that it was like no dog they had ever seen before. It had flippers for legs, a fish's tail, and the body of a dolphin. And it was badly hurt.

Manu tried to calm the animal. He brought cool water and cleaned the wound. He built a shelter against the sun and kept the fur wet with seawater.

The brothers left Manu. They had no time for an animal that was going to die. They had to prepare for the long sea voyage home.

> **STOP AND THINK**
>
> **Question** What kind of animal have the brothers found? Why does Manu help it? What do you think will happen if the animal lives?

But the animal didn't die.

"I will call you 'Dog-of-the-Sea-Waves,'" Manu said on the third day, as he fed him fish.

At the end of the week, the two had their first swim together, and before long, they were playing tag in the waves. Manu made up a silly chant:

Dog-of-the-Sea-Waves,
Dog-with-no-paws,
Dog-with-no-ears,
Dog-with-no-wag,
We're friends!

Granulated Cowry

Manu giggled, and Dog-of-the-Sea-Waves tickled his cheek with his whiskers.

"Come help me dry berries and roots for the voyage home," called Hōkū.

"We need fish," scolded Nāʻale.

"There's water to gather," scowled ʻŌpua.

"And sails to repair," cried Makani.

But Manu pretended not to hear. Instead he and Dog-of-the-Sea-Waves played together and got into all kinds of trouble. They terrorized the fish Nāʻale was trying to catch. They made a mess of the beach where Hōkū was drying food. They played with Makani's ropes and accidentally pulled ʻŌpua's gourds off the boat, tripping Makani, who fell into the water.

No one laughed. The two were separated, and Manu was put to work.

Manu gathered berries for Hōkū. He caught fish for Nāʻale. He fetched water for ʻŌpua. He twisted rope for Makani. But every evening after his work was done, he slipped off to meet his friend, and they played in the waves until it got too dark to see. Then Manu swam ashore, and Dog-of-the-Sea-Waves went hunting for food.

After many months of hard work, the boat was finally ready to leave. At the last moment, Manu dived into the water to say goodbye to Dog-of-the-Sea-Waves. As the brothers yelled for Manu to get aboard, Dog-of-the-Sea-Waves brushed his whiskers against Manu's cheek, then disappeared beneath the waves.

Hawaiian Raspberry

The brothers sailed down the island chain. When they came to the last island, 'Ōpua said, "Is that a cloud on the side of that mountain, or smoke? Let's go see."

Curious, the brothers anchored their boat in a quiet bay and swam ashore.

Halfway up the mountain, Makani felt a warm wind and hesitated. But his brothers told him not to worry.

After a few more steps, Manu noticed that the birds were silent. But his brothers paid no attention.

Then—a jolt!

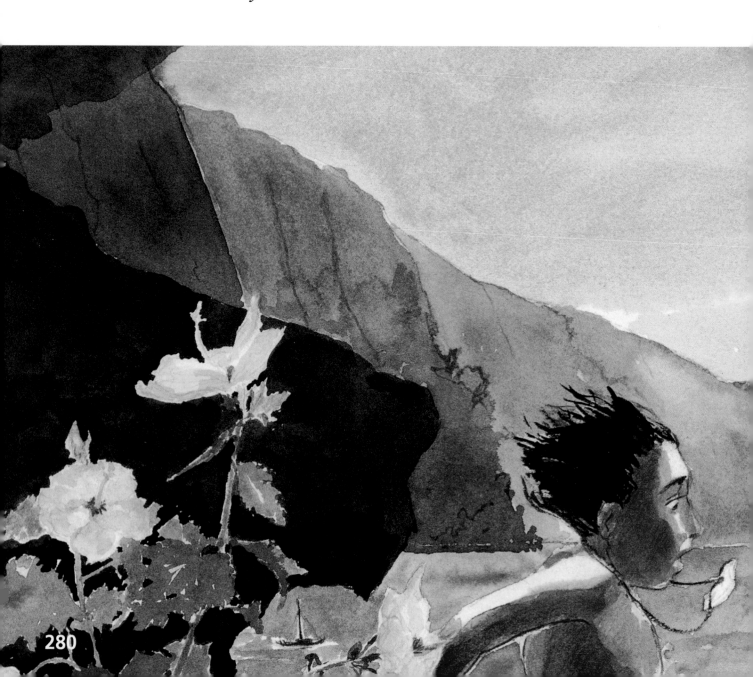

The earth heaved up and slammed the brothers to the ground. Deep cracks appeared, then flames.

Hōkū grabbed Manu's hand, and the brothers fled down the slope. But a river of fire cut them off from the sea and forced them to the cliffs.

The earth shuddered, and the five brothers jumped—into the sea far below.

Wekiu Bug

But the sea they landed in was a monster. It thrashed from the earthquakes. It hissed from the burning lava. It lashed out at the brothers and grabbed Manu. In an instant, he was gone.

Makani filled his lungs with air and went to the very depths of the ocean, but there was no sign of Manu. 'Ōpua, with his voice like thunder, shouted for Manu above the crashing waves, but there was no answer. Nā'ale, who loved the sea, begged it to be calm, but it wouldn't listen.

Dragon Moray

STOP AND THINK

Author's Craft What comparison does the author make to create a picture in your mind of how the sea looked, felt, and sounded?

TEKS 3.10 ELPS 4F

All this time, Manu was fighting to get to the surface, but the sea wouldn't let go. Then he felt the whiskers. Manu clasped his arms around Dog-of-the-Sea-Waves, and up they went.

Pompom Crab

It was Hōkū who spotted them. The brothers raced
toward Manu and cradled him above the waves.

"Manu, Manu," they cried over and over as they made
their way to the boat. And to Dog-of-the-Sea-Waves they
chanted their thanks:

Dog-that-swims-the-depths,
Dog-that-braves-the-currents,
Dog-that-knows-the-sea,
Dog-that-cares-for-our-brother.

The brothers then weighed anchor and headed for the
southern sea and home. Manu stood on the deck and
listened to Dog-of-the-Sea-Waves barking goodbye.
"We'll be back," Manu shouted.

Happyface Spider

And when they returned, they came with their families. They embraced the land and made it their home.

✔ **STOP AND THINK**

Author's Purpose Tell in your own words what you think the author wants readers to learn from the brothers' story.

TEKS 3.5A

1. Which word from page 275 means the opposite of the word <u>departure</u>?

   ⬭ *arrival*

   ⬭ *voyage*

   ⬭ *home*

   ⬭ *sails*

   TEKS 3.4C

2. ✔ TARGET SKILL **Author's Purpose**

   List details on a chart like this that show how Manu and Dog-of-the-Sea-Waves work, play, and care for each other. Then tell the author's opinion of whether humans and animals can truly be friends. **TEKS** RC-3(D)

3. ✔ TARGET STRATEGY **Question**

   Ask yourself questions about the story, such as, What have I learned? What questions were left unanswered? **TEKS** 3.2B

4. **Oral Language** Use the Retelling Cards to talk to a partner about the brothers' experience. Do not speak too loudly or too softly. **TEKS** 3.30

   Retelling Cards

 TEKS 3.2B ask questions/clarify/locate facts/details/use text evidence; **3.4C** identify/use antonyms/synonyms/homographs/homophones; **3.30** speak coherently/effectively about topics; **RC-3(D)** make inferences/use textual evidence

The Land Volcanoes Built

GENRE

Informational text gives factual information about a topic. This is a magazine article.

TEXT FOCUS

A **diagram** is a drawing that shows how something works. Examine the diagram on page 289. Then explain to a partner the steps that lead to a volcanic eruption.

TEKS 3.15A follow/explain written directions **ELPS** 3H narrate/describe/explain with detail

The Land Volcanoes Built

by Patricia Ann Lynch

The islands of Hawaii spread over many miles of ocean. Eight large islands and 124 small ones are in the chain.

Each island is really the top of a mountain that pokes out of the sea. How were these islands formed? The answer is *volcanoes*.

What Is a Volcano?

A volcano is an opening, or vent, that goes deep into Earth. Deep within Earth it is so hot that rock melts. The melted rock is called magma.

Sometimes magma is pushed up and pours out of the volcano. Then the magma is called lava. The lava cools and hardens. It builds up. Over time, it can form a tall mountain. Each of the Hawaiian Islands formed in this way.

A Volcano Erupts

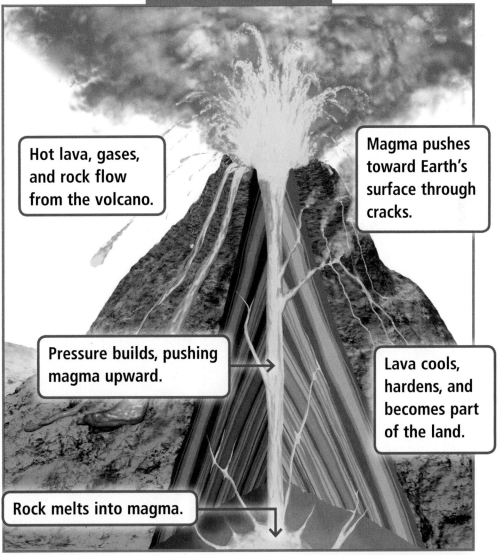

Hot lava, gases, and rock flow from the volcano.

Magma pushes toward Earth's surface through cracks.

Pressure builds, pushing magma upward.

Lava cools, hardens, and becomes part of the land.

Rock melts into magma.

Life Arrives

At first, the islands were bare. Waves rippled on empty shores. Life came much later. Wind and water carried plant seeds. Sea animals such as monk seals swam there. Other animals made the voyage aboard objects floating in the sea. The arrival of birds brought song.

The first people paddled in canoes from other islands. The stars guided them across the Pacific Ocean. The travelers spotted the islands. They dropped anchor in a calm bay and came ashore. The new islands were good places to live. There was plenty of fresh water to drink and lots of food. The leaves of the coconut tree could be used to build thatched shelters. Coconut husks could be twisted into strong ropes. These people became the first Hawaiians.

People from China, Japan, Samoa, the Philippines, and other countries live in Hawaii today.

Making Connections

 Text to Self   TEKS RC-3(F)

Draw a Picture Imagine you are a brother in *Dog-of-the-Sea-Waves*. Draw a picture of what you might see when you arrive at one of the islands. Use the text and pictures from *Dog-of-the-Sea-Waves* and "The Land Volcanoes Built" for ideas.

 Text to Text   TEKS 3.30, RC-3(F) ELPS 3E

Connect to Science Find sections in *Dog-of-the-Sea-Waves* that refer to volcanoes or their effects. Use what you learned in "The Land Volcanoes Built" to explain to a partner what was really happening during that passage.

 Text to World   TEKS 3.26A(ii)

Volcano Hunt Besides Hawaii, where are volcanoes found around the world? Do research on the Internet or in reference books. Share your findings with the class.

 TEKS **3.26A(ii)** collect information from experts/reference texts/online searches; **3.30** speak coherently/effectively about topics; **RC-3(F)** make connections between texts; **ELPS 3E** share information in cooperative learning interactions

Grammar

What Is an Adverb? An adverb is a word that describes a verb. Adverbs can tell *how, when,* or *where* an action happens. Adverbs can come before or after the verbs they describe.

Academic Language

adverb

Kim saw a seal at the zoo yesterday. (tells *when*)

She carefully touched the seal's belly. (tells *how*)

The seal eats there. (tells *where*)

It barked loudly. (tells *how*)

 Work with a partner. Read the sentences aloud. Find the adverb in each sentence.

❶ Alex ran ahead.

❷ He reached the beach first.

❸ He eagerly searched for the seal.

❹ He looked everywhere for his friend.

❺ Alex found the seal playing quietly in the ocean.

292

Sentence Fluency Short, choppy sentences can be combined to make your writing smoother. Combine two sentences by moving an adverb. Often you can choose where to place the adverb in the new sentence.

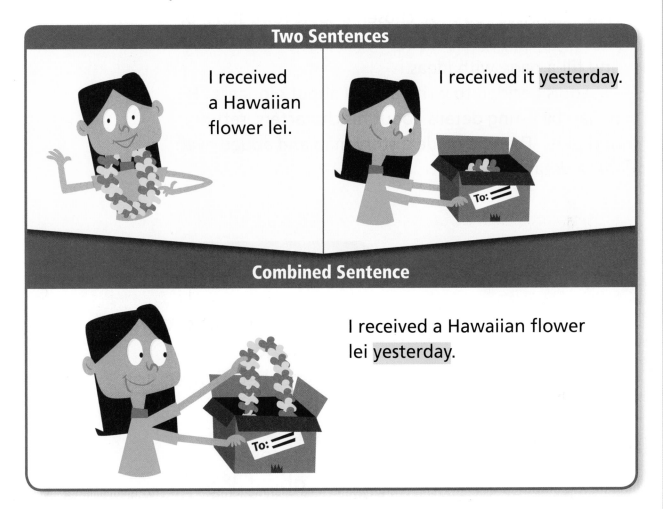

Two Sentences

I received a Hawaiian flower lei.

I received it yesterday.

Combined Sentence

I received a Hawaiian flower lei yesterday.

Two sentences:	A lei should be draped over the shoulders. A lei should be draped gently.
Combined sentence:	A lei should be draped gently over the shoulders.

Connect Grammar to Writing

As you revise your story next week, think about combining sentences by moving an adverb.

Reading-Writing Workshop Prewriting
Write to Express

☑ **Ideas** Once you have chosen a topic for a story, or **fictional narrative**, explore your topic. Think about it and fill a page with ideas.

Louis decided to write a story about pioneers. He began by listing details about his characters, setting, and plot. Then he made a story map and added even more details.

Writing Process Checklist

▶ **Prewriting**

☑ **Did I pick a topic that my audience and I will enjoy?**

☑ **Did I decide what my characters and setting are like?**

☑ **Did I plan a good beginning, middle, and end?**

☑ **Did I think of enough details?**

Drafting

Revising

Proofreading

Publishing

Exploring a Topic

Who?   a family in a covered wagon
mother, father, son

Where and when?   a desert
about 1850

What?   get stuck in a sandstorm
water supply running low

294

Story Map

Setting	Characters
the desert, during a sandstorm inside a covered wagon, hot, crowded with furniture	Sam: scared, tired of waiting Ma: hopeful Pop: calm, cheerful, good storyteller

Plot

Beginning Sam and his family have been stuck in a sandstorm for ten hours.

Middle Sam is hot, scared that they will run out of water.

Pop tells him not to worry. Ma talks about their new home out West.

End Pop tells Sam a story.

Pop's story helps Sam relax until the storm ends.

> **When I organized my fictional narrative, I added more details.**

Reading as a Writer

Which of Louis's details help you picture what is happening? What details can you add to your own chart to make the plot clear?

Lesson 25

✓ TARGET VOCABULARY

approached

section

avalanches

increases

equipment

tanks

slopes

altitude

succeed

halt

Vocabulary Reader

Context Cards

ELPS 1D speak using learning strategies

Vocabulary in Context

1. approached

Climbers **approached** this mountain from the west. Slowly, they got nearer to it.

2. section

The top **section**, or part, of this mountain is the steepest.

3. avalanches

When **avalanches** occur, the powerful sliding snow can knock trees down.

4. increases

When storms blow in, the danger to climbers **increases**, or becomes greater.

- **Study each Context Card.**
- **Ask a question that uses one of the Vocabulary words.**

5 equipment

Mountain climbers check their supplies, or equipment, before a climb.

6 tanks

Tanks that hold oxygen help climbers breathe in the high, thin air.

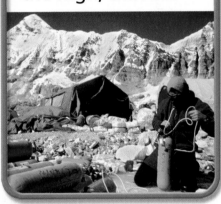

7 slopes

Gentle slopes near the bottom of the mountain are easiest to climb.

8 altitude

The altitude, or height, of Granite Peak in Montana is 12,799 feet high.

9 succeed

Everyone's goal is to reach the summit. If climbers plan well, they will succeed!

10 halt

Climbers come to a halt when it gets dark. They stop for the night.

Background

✓ TARGET VOCABULARY **Mountain Climbing** Mountain peaks may look beautiful from far away, but they can also be deadly. Climbers should prepare long before the slopes are approached. Improper equipment increases the chances of a climb coming to a dangerous halt.

Smart climbers use maps showing each section of the mountain. They may also require special safety equipment to survive avalanches. Oxygen tanks for breathing at high altitude may also be needed. Climbers who have planned well are most likely to succeed!

ice ax
helmet
ice anchor
rope
windbreaker
harness
backpack
carabiner
boots with crampons
snow pants

Comprehension

✔ TARGET SKILL Text and Graphic Features

As you read *Mountains: Surviving on Mt. Everest*, pay
attention to the text, charts, and other graphic features
the author uses to help make the information clear. Use
a chart like this one to list the text and graphic features
in this selection. Tell why you think the author uses them.

Text or Graphic Feature	Page	Purpose

✔ TARGET STRATEGY Infer/Predict

Text and graphic features, such as headings, captions,
and charts, can help you predict which details are more
important to the selection. Look at the text and graphic
features to predict what the author considers important.

Main Selection

Mountains
Surviving on Mt. Everest

TARGET VOCABULARY

approached	tanks
section	slopes
avalanches	altitude
increases	succeed
equipment	halt

TARGET SKILL

Text and Graphic Features Tell how words and photos work together.

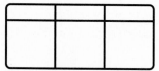

TARGET STRATEGY

Infer/Predict Use text and graphic clues to figure out more about the selection.

GENRE

Informational text gives factual information about a topic.

TEKS 3.2B ask questions/clarify/locate facts/details/use text evidence **ELPS 4D** use prereading supports to comprehend texts

MEET THE AUTHOR

Michael Sandler

Michael Sandler enjoys extreme adventures. He loves to travel and has been to the foothills of Mount Everest, the highest mountain in the world. Several years ago while touring Africa, he got lost in the Sahara, the world's largest desert. That adventure might have helped him later to write *Deserts: Surviving in the Sahara*.

Other extreme books by Sandler include *Oceans: Surviving in the Deep Sea* and *Rain Forests: Surviving in the Amazon*.

300

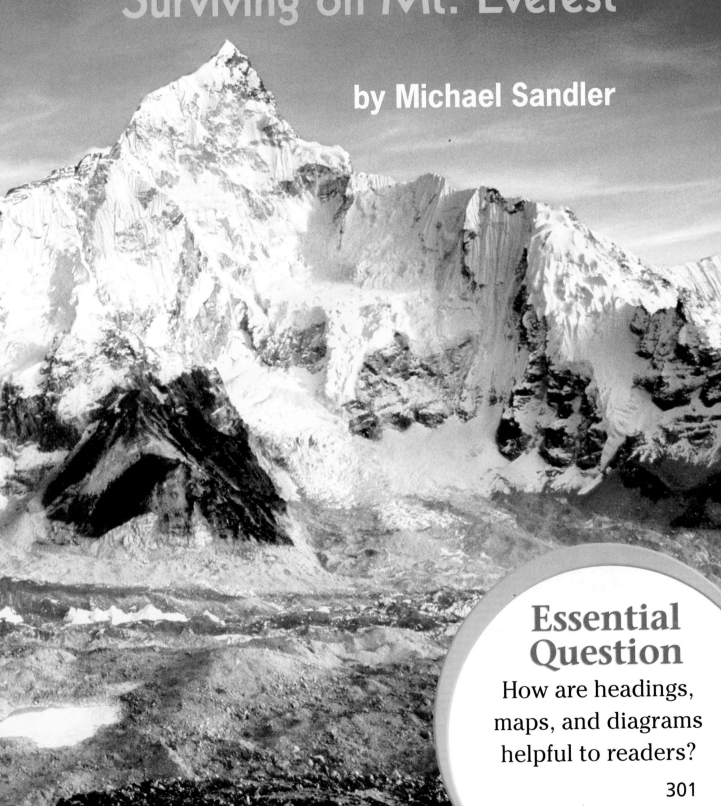

Mountains
Surviving on Mt. Everest

by Michael Sandler

Climbing Mount Everest

The clock showed almost midnight. The temperature was freezing. Icy winds roared by.

A group of people huddled in the darkness on a rocky ridge. In moments, they would begin the final stage of a dangerous journey. They were climbing to the top of Mount Everest, the world's highest mountain.

Among the climbers was Temba Tsheri (SHUHR ee) Sherpa. Just two weeks before, Temba had celebrated his 16th birthday. Now he was trying to survive in one of the world's most extreme places. Making it to the top of Everest was Temba's dream. He would be the youngest person ever to reach the summit, which is 29,035 feet (8,850 meters) high.

What Are Mountains?

Mountains are a type of tall landform. They rise high above the area around them. Mountains are taller than hills. They can rise thousands of feet (kilometers) in the air. They are found all over the world, even beneath the sea.

A group of mountains is called a range. The biggest mountain range in North America is the Rocky Mountains. The Andes (AN deez), in South America, is the world's longest mountain range.

ARCTIC OCEAN

ASIA

NORTH
ATLANTIC
OCEAN

EUROPE

Alps

Rocky
Mountains

NORTH
PACIFIC
OCEAN

NORTH
AMERICA

Atlas
Mountains

NORTH
PACIFIC
OCEAN

AFRICA

Himalaya
Mountains

Andes
Mountains

SOUTH
AMERICA

East Africa
Mountains

AUSTRALIA

SOUTH PACIFIC OCEAN

SOUTH
ATLANTIC
OCEAN

INDIAN OCEAN

Great
Dividing
Range

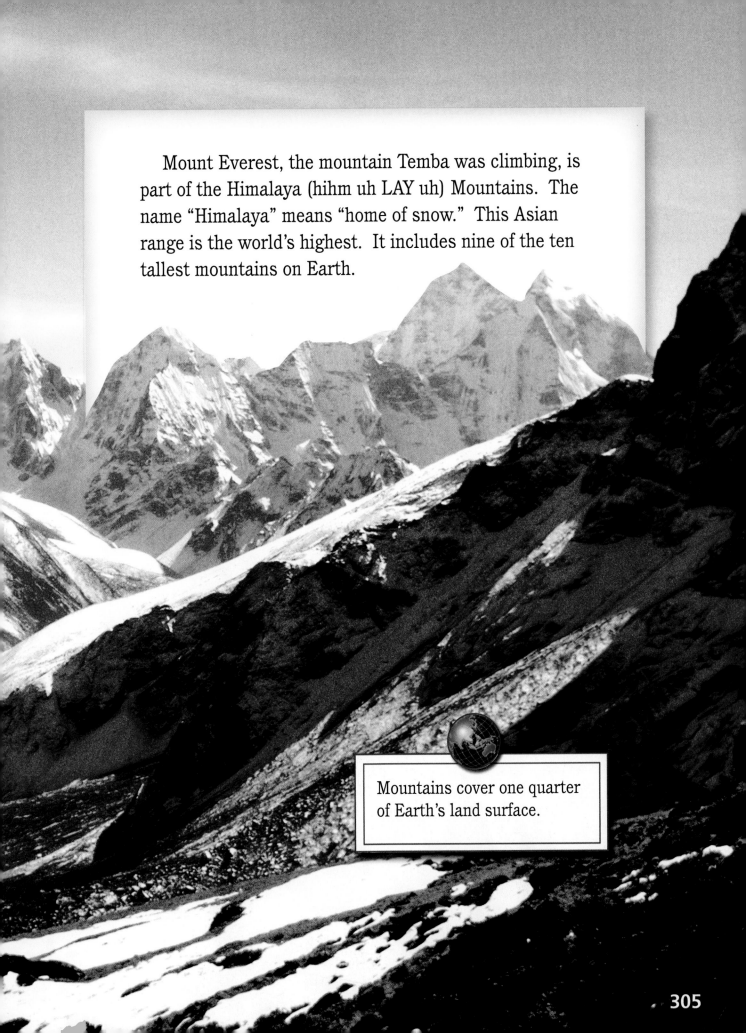

Mount Everest, the mountain Temba was climbing, is part of the Himalaya (hihm uh LAY uh) Mountains. The name "Himalaya" means "home of snow." This Asian range is the world's highest. It includes nine of the ten tallest mountains on Earth.

Mountains cover one quarter of Earth's land surface.

Mountain Conditions

As Temba approached Everest's summit, survival became harder and harder. Mountain conditions get more extreme the higher a person climbs.

Air contains less and less oxygen as the altitude increases. Breathing becomes nearly impossible. Thin air can cause headaches and dizziness at 10,000 feet (3,048 meters). Higher up, it can be deadly.

Humans cannot survive for long at the top section of mountains like Everest. Hurricane-force winds can reach 130 miles per hour (209 kph). Temperatures can plummet to −100F (−73C) during the night. Blowing snow makes it hard to see. Temba was headed here.

Frostbite can happen when it's so cold that hands, feet, and other parts of the body freeze solid. Frostbite can cause people to lose fingers, toes—even their noses.

Why Do People Climb Mountains?

People climb mountains for many reasons. Some enjoy the thrill of being high above the clouds. Others like the challenge of testing their skills.

For decades, however, reaching the top of Everest was a test that no climber could pass. The first attempts to climb Everest were made during the 1920s. Again and again, the climbing teams stopped short of their goal. Avalanches, storms, sickness, and exhaustion brought them to a halt.

Then, in 1953, two climbers finally succeeded— Sir Edmund Hillary and Tenzing Norgay. Sir Hillary was from New Zealand. Norgay was a Sherpa from Nepal (nuh PAWL).

> ✔ **STOP AND THINK**
>
> **Text and Graphic Features** These pages include headings, a caption, and a boxed fact. What kinds of information do these text features provide?
>
> **TEKS** 3.13D **ELPS** 4F

Sir Edmund Hillary (left) and Tenzing Norgay (right) show off their survival equipment in 1953.

Temba's Mistake

Temba had tried to climb Everest before. It ended, however, in failure.

"I didn't have enough training or proper equipment," Temba said. He was almost at the summit when his oxygen supply ran out.

Without oxygen, Temba couldn't think clearly. He made a terrible mistake. He took off his gloves to tie his boots. His fingers froze. Temba suffered frostbite on both hands. He had to turn back just 70 feet (21 meters) from his goal.

The next time around, however, Temba was prepared. He had trained hard. He had the right equipment, thanks to his classmates and teachers. They had raised money for his trip.

Survival Equipment

CLIMBING SUIT—to protect against cold

GLOVES—to keep hands warm and dry

GOGGLES—to protect eyes from the sun's harmful rays and from reflection off snow

OXYGEN MASK AND TANK—for breathing at the highest altitudes

ICE AX—to help climb slopes and break up ice

CLIMBING ROPES—to climb up slopes

TREKKING POLES—to help a climber stay balanced

MOUNTAIN BOOTS—with spikes that dig into the snow and ice

Camp-to-Camp

Temba's second try began in April 2001. Mount Everest sits between Nepal and Tibet (tuh BEHT). There are several different routes to the top. Temba would take a route from the north, the Tibetan side.

Climbers move from one camp to the next higher one and then rest for a while. At each camp, their bodies get used to the higher altitudes. Temba spent several weeks moving between camps with his team.

At Camp 3, the team waited for a break in the weather. Winter was over, but there had been a series of severe snowstorms. Getting caught in a snowstorm farther up the mountain would be deadly.

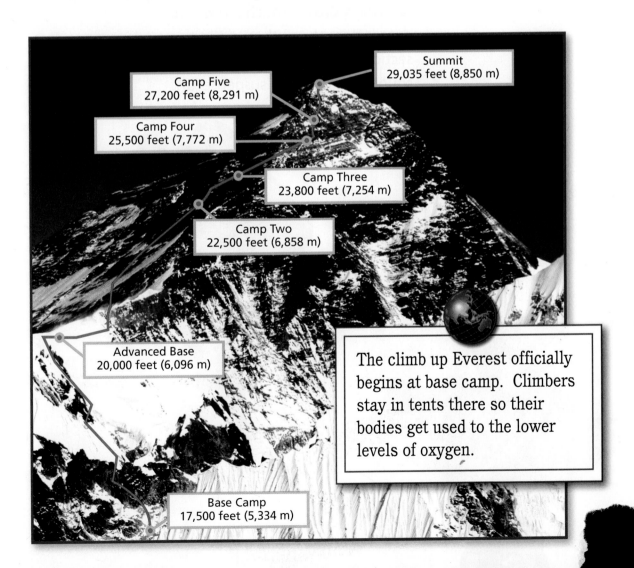

Summit
29,035 feet (8,850 m)

Camp Five
27,200 feet (8,291 m)

Camp Four
25,500 feet (7,772 m)

Camp Three
23,800 feet (7,254 m)

Camp Two
22,500 feet (6,858 m)

Advanced Base
20,000 feet (6,096 m)

The climb up Everest officially begins at base camp. Climbers stay in tents there so their bodies get used to the lower levels of oxygen.

Base Camp
17,500 feet (5,334 m)

The Climb Along the Ridge

On May 20, Temba's team reached Camp 4. Then the climbers headed out on the great ridge leading to the summit. Temba plunged his ax into ice walls, pulling himself up. He steadied himself against 50-mile-per-hour (80-kph) winds. Yet, he climbed higher and higher.

Temba had to move fast or die. Darkness stopped him before he got to Camp 5. His team had gone ahead. Luckily, Temba found a tent. He spent the night frightened and alone.

The next day, Temba rejoined his team. They reached Camp 6, one day's climb from their goal.

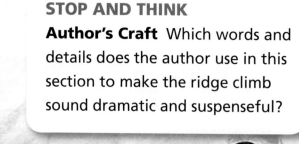

STOP AND THINK

Author's Craft Which words and details does the author use in this section to make the ridge climb sound dramatic and suspenseful?

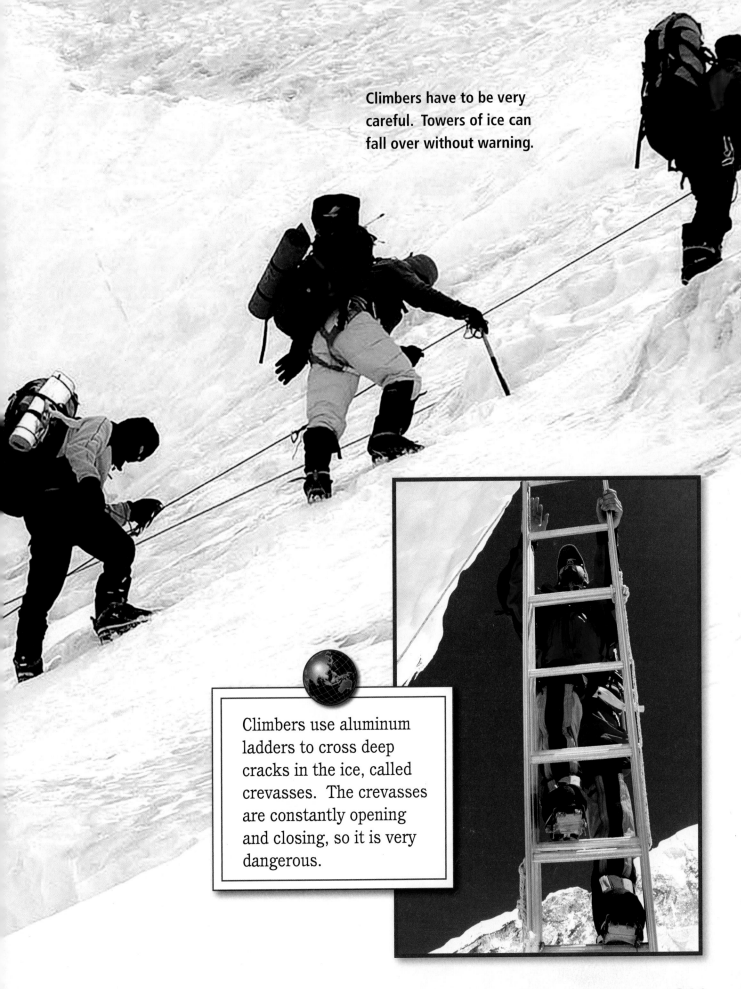

Climbers have to be very careful. Towers of ice can fall over without warning.

Climbers use aluminum ladders to cross deep cracks in the ice, called crevasses. The crevasses are constantly opening and closing, so it is very dangerous.

Reaching the Top of the World

Just before midnight, Temba began his final climb. A headlamp lit the darkness. An oxygen mask helped Temba to breathe. Sometimes he'd stop to rest or to change oxygen bottles.

Just after sunrise, Temba reached Mount Everest's summit. He was higher than anyone else on the planet. Temba planted two flags. One was for his school. The other was for Nepal.
"I felt so happy," he said.

It is dangerous for climbers to spend more than ten minutes at the top of Everest. The body needs to get to a lower altitude where there is more oxygen.

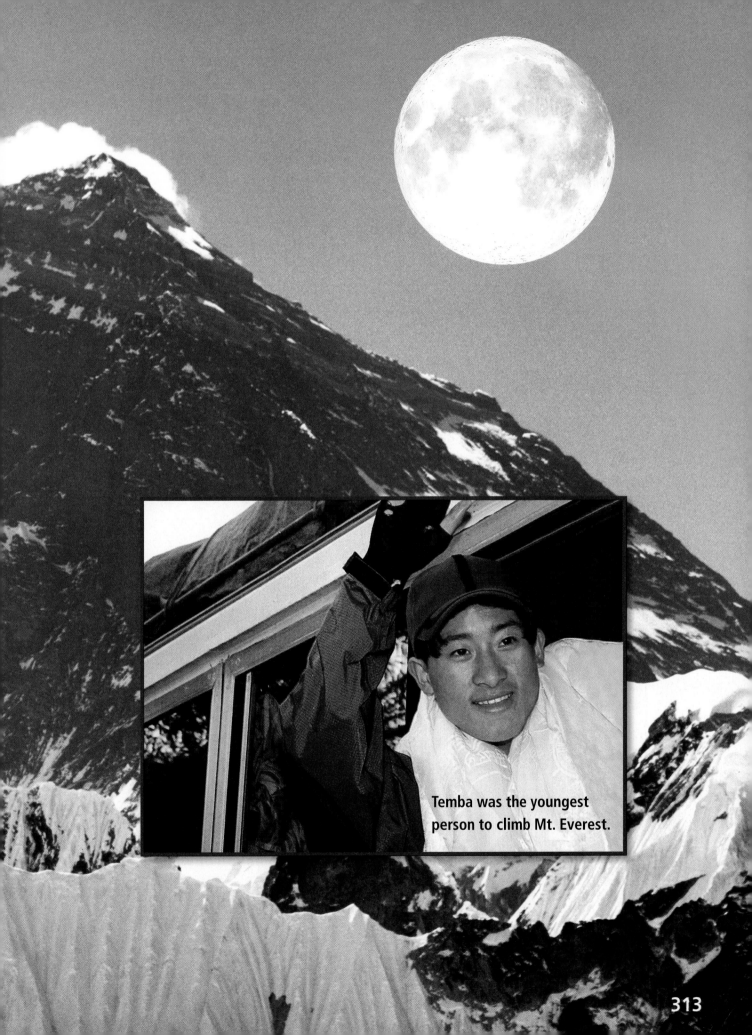

Temba was the youngest person to climb Mt. Everest.

Will the Mountains Survive?

Temba survived in the mountains. Now, he wants to make sure the mountains survive. The world's mountains face many different threats.

Trash is one problem. For a while, Everest was called the "world's highest garbage dump." The mountain was littered with tons of trash that climbers left behind—batteries, bottles, and empty oxygen tanks. Many climbers didn't have the time or strength to carry these things back down with them.

Climbers have left garbage on Everest since 1921. Now, people are trying to clean up the mess.

Global warming is another problem. As Earth gets warmer, mountain glaciers are melting. Himalayan lakes are swelling up with water. When they flood, mountain landscapes will be changed forever.

 STOP AND THINK

Infer/Predict The author says Temba wants the mountains to survive. What do you think this means? What questions would you ask Temba to find out?

TEKS 3.2B

In 2005, the snowcap on Tanzania's Mount Kilimanjaro melted for the first time in history.

315

After the Climb

When Temba came down from Everest, he was thinking about food, not fame. After weeks of camping, he was starving for home cooking.

Still, when he flew home to Kathmandu, a huge crowd was waiting. Temba couldn't believe it. "I had never seen so many cameras.... All of them were pointed at me," he said.

Despite the attention, Temba focused on his schoolwork. He needed a good education to achieve his other dream, starting a school in Dolakha.

Will Temba succeed? Only time will tell. If you've survived on Everest, however, and reached the top, no goal seems too high!

Kathmandu (kat man DOO) is the capital and largest city of Nepal.

Temba smiled at supporters who greeted him at the Kathmandu airport after he successfully climbed Mt. Everest.

1. On page 306, the word <u>approached</u> means —

   ⬭ left

   ⬭ neared

   ⬭ saw

   ⬭ ended

2. ✔ **TARGET SKILL** **Text and Graphic Features**

   Pick three photos from the selection. Use a chart like this to list where each photo is found. Tell what the photos show and why you think the author used them. **TEKS** 3.15B; **ELPS** 4F

3. ✔ **TARGET STRATEGY** **Infer/Predict**

   Reread the section, "Will the Mountains Survive" on page 314. Why do you think the author included this section? What might the author want readers to think or do? **TEKS** 3.14

4. **Oral Language** Use the Retelling Cards to describe Temba's climb up Mt. Everest. Describe the events in order. Look at the class when you speak. **TEKS** 3.30; RC-3(E)

Retelling Cards

 TEKS 3.14 identify author's persuasion; **3.15B** locate/use graphic features of text; **3.30** speak coherently/effectively about topics; RC-3(E) summarize information in text; **ELPS** 4F use visual/contextual/peer/teacher support to read/comprehend texts

Connect to

Plays

THE
BIG
CLEANUP

✓ **TARGET VOCABULARY**

approached	tanks
section	slopes
avalanches	altitude
increases	succeed
equipment	halt

GENRE

A **play** tells a story through the words and actions of characters. After you read *The Big Cleanup*, discuss the story problem and what the characters do to try to solve this problem. Explain how Scott's words show that he is a leader.

TEXT FOCUS

Stage directions in plays give information about the characters and setting.

 TEKS 3.7 explain plot/character through dialogue in scripts;

THE BIG CLEANUP

by Kate McGovern

Cast of Characters

Scott, leader of the "Clean Everest" team
Talia, a team member
Rinzen, a guide from a nearby village

(A special team is preparing to climb Mt. Everest.)

Scott: Many people love to climb Mount Everest, but they leave behind trash. We're a new kind of climbing team. We're going up Mount Everest to help clean it up. Does everyone have his or her equipment?

Talia: (holding up her trash bags) We do. These bags are for carrying down trash.

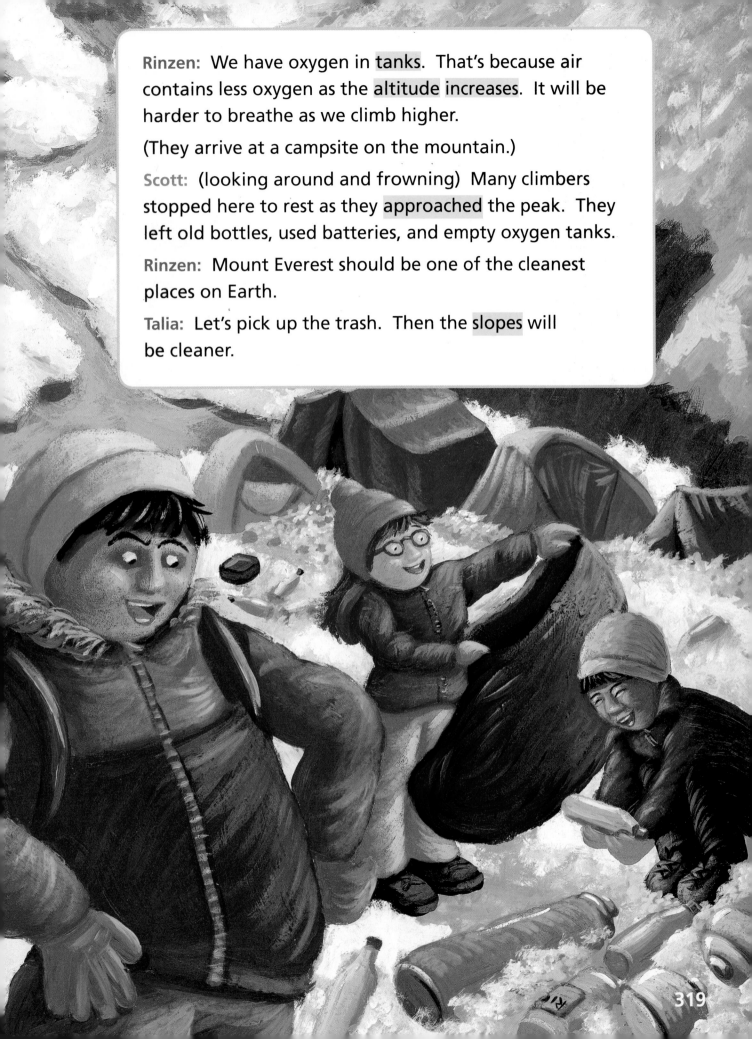

Rinzen: We have oxygen in tanks. That's because air contains less oxygen as the altitude increases. It will be harder to breathe as we climb higher.

(They arrive at a campsite on the mountain.)

Scott: (looking around and frowning) Many climbers stopped here to rest as they approached the peak. They left old bottles, used batteries, and empty oxygen tanks.

Rinzen: Mount Everest should be one of the cleanest places on Earth.

Talia: Let's pick up the trash. Then the slopes will be cleaner.

319

Talia: We must be careful of avalanches up here.

Rinzen: That's right. An avalanche would bring our work to a halt.

Scott: (waving them onward) Let's go! This is the last section to climb. When we succeed, we will have climbed the tallest mountain on Earth.

Talia: We'll have collected lots of trash.

Scott: Other people are helping to clean Mount Everest, too. These days, climbers must bring drinks in cans. Then they flatten the empty cans and carry them away in their backpacks. If we all do our part, Mount Everest can stay clean for a long time.

Making Connections

Climbing a Mountain Would you like to climb Mt. Everest like Temba in *Mountains* or the characters in *The Big Cleanup*? Why or why not? Take turns telling a partner. Listen to each other and ask questions.

Write a Play With a small group, write and act out your own short play in the style of *The Big Cleanup* about cleaning up trash on Mt. Everest. Include two facts from *Mountains* in your play.

Connect to Math Use details from *Mountains* to figure out how many years it was from the time Sir Edmund Hillary climbed Mt. Everest to the time Temba did. Hillary was born on July 20, 1919. How old was he when Temba reached the top of Mt. Everest?

Grammar

What Is a Preposition? A **preposition** connects words in a sentence. Prepositions can tell *where* or *when*. A **prepositional phrase** is a group of words that includes a preposition, a noun or pronoun, and words that describe that noun or pronoun.

Academic Language

preposition

prepositional phrase

Preposition	Prepositional Phrase
below	The clouds sit below the mountaintop.
during	The hiker lost eight pounds during the climb.
to	The climbers hike to the peak.
until	Temba waited until the storm passed.

 Circle the preposition. Then underline the prepositional phrase in each sentence.

1. Marty climbed up the long hill.

2. A heavy rain started during the hike.

3. Marty rested under some trees.

4. It was dry inside his tent.

5. He finished the hike by lunchtime.

Sentence Fluency Short, choppy sentences can be combined to make your writing smoother. You can combine two sentences by moving a prepositional phrase.

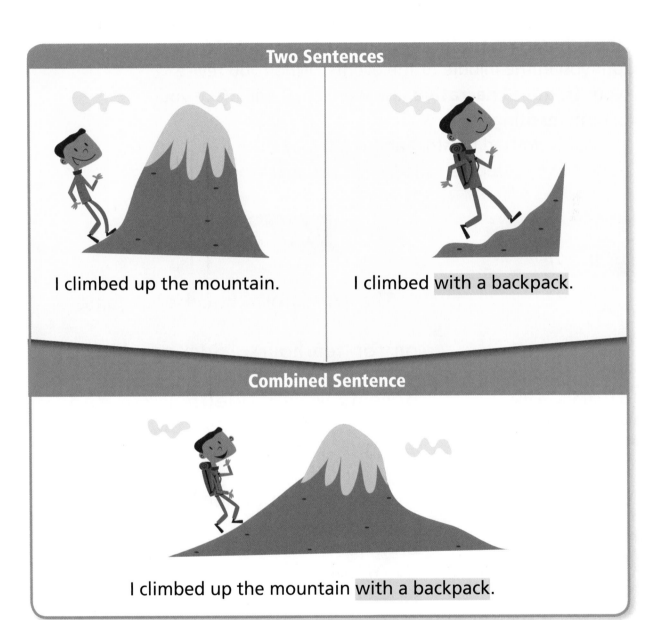

Two Sentences

I climbed up the mountain.

I climbed with a backpack.

Combined Sentence

I climbed up the mountain with a backpack.

✏️ **Grammar in Writing**

As you revise your story, look for places where you can combine sentences by moving a prepositional phrase.

Reading-Writing Workshop: Revise

Write to Express

☑ **Word Choice** Good writers try to make you feel what their characters are feeling. They use strong words to put you in the middle of the events. When you revise your **fictional narrative**, use words that will make your writing exciting.

Louis drafted his story about a family stuck in a sandstorm. Later, he added some stronger words.

Writing Process Checklist

Prewrite

Draft

▶ **Revise**

☑ Did I introduce the characters, setting, and problem in an interesting way?

☑ Does the middle part show how the characters deal with the problem?

☑ Does the end show how the problem works out?

☑ Did I use vivid words, details, and dialogue?

Edit

Publish and Share

Revised Draft

The sandstorm had been going on for ten hours. Sam and his parents ~~were~~ hid inside their covered wagon. The wind blew faster and louder than Sam ever remembered. ~~It blew louder too.~~ The sand was ~~moving~~ whipping around them.

Sam and his family were moving out West.

Sandstorm!

by Louis Hudson

The sandstorm had been going on for ten hours. Sam and his parents hid inside their covered wagon. The wind blew faster and louder than Sam ever remembered. The sand was whipping around them.

Sam and his family were moving out West. Their wagon was full of everything they owned. There was barely enough room to sit. With the flaps closed, it was hot and stuffy inside. Sam poked his sweaty head out, but the sand stung him like insects. "How long will we have to wait?" he asked. His voice was shaky.

> In my final paper, I used stronger words to show how my characters felt. I also combined sentences.

Reading as a Writer

Which words show how Sam feels? Where can you make changes in your story to show what your characters are experiencing?

> Read both selections. Then read the questions that follow them. Decide which is the best answer to each question.

A Great Idea

1   "Mom's birthday is soon," Anne said to her brothers. "What should we give her?"

2   "We have to think of something different to make for her," said Carl. "We have written poems, stories, and songs. I'm almost out of ideas."

> 1.   Make twelve calendar pages.
> 2.   Put family photos on each page.
> 3.   Write in birthdays and fun holidays.
> 4.   Wrap the gift and make a card.

3   "I know!" yelled Danny. "Let's make a calendar for Mom."

4   "That's a great idea," said Anne. "We can make it a special calendar all about our family. It will take some effort. Before we begin, let's make a list of the work that needs to be done. It is important to make a plan if we want this done right."

5   The children decided who would do each job. Danny would print the calendar pages. Anne would write the birthdays. Carl would write holidays. All three would pick family pictures.

6   They would make the card together, too. Anne would wrap the gift. They would keep their jobs a secret from Mom.

7   The next day, the children went to the library with Mom. Anne asked Mom to help her choose a book from the children's section. Meanwhile, Danny found free calendar pages online and printed them. Carl searched the Internet and made a list of fun holidays, such as National Hugging Day.

8   When they got home, Anne made a list of all the birthdays. Next, the children went through their family photos. For March, they chose a picture of the family flying kites at the park. For July, they used beach pictures from past summer vacations. They found pictures to use for every month.

GO ON ➤

9 Now they were ready to put everything together. They pasted the pictures on the calendar pages. Then they wrote in the birthdays and holidays. When they finished, Anne wrapped the calendar. They made a card and signed it.

10 The children got up early on Mom's birthday. She was still in bed when they gave her the gift. Mom unwrapped the calendar. She looked at every picture and read every word. She laughed at the funny holidays. "This is so wonderful!" she said. "I don't know what to say."

11 "Look at this month's page," said Carl. "It will tell you what to say!"

12 Mom looked at the calendar. "January is National Thank-You Month," she read aloud. "Well, thank you very much. This is a gift from the heart that will last all year!"

The Big Day

1 It seemed to Maria that her whole family was acting ridiculous. It was all because of her sister Lucy's fifteenth birthday. Maria's parents were born in Mexico. It was a Mexican tradition to have a big party for a girl turning fifteen. The celebration was called a *Quinceaños*.

2 At first Maria was excited about the party. They were going to have a tent outside, and a band. Maria's grandparents were coming from Mexico. Lucy said everything was going to be awesome. But Maria started thinking it would be awesome when the party was over.

3 Planning the party took so much work! Maria was organized, so she was in charge of gathering addresses for the invitations. She also made beautiful decorations. But she felt as if no one noticed.

4 In the meantime, Maria had important things going on, too. She scored her first goal in soccer. She got an A on a spelling test. She was elected class secretary. Usually her family would celebrate those things with her. Now she didn't bother telling them her news. She thought they would just disregard her. They seemed to ignore everything else she did.

5 One night Maria heard a knock on her bedroom door. It was Lucy.

6 "Hi Maria," Lucy said. "Come with me. I have something to show you."

7 "Look what I bought with my babysitting money," Lucy said. She reached into her closet.

8   Lucy put a small box on her bed. Maria opened it and lifted out a beautiful necklace made of tiny glass beads.

9   "I got it for you!" said Lucy. "You have been so helpful with my party, and I haven't even asked what's going on in your life lately. This is my way of saying sorry and thank you!"

10   Maria smiled and tried on her new necklace. It was perfect. More importantly, her sister *had* noticed her. Maria was starting to think this party was going to be awesome after all.

> **Use "A Great Idea" and "The Big Day"**
> **to answer questions 1–4.**

1   In paragraph 4 of "The Big Day," which word helps the reader know what the word disregard means?

⬭ *bother*

⬭ *celebrate*

⬭ *tell*

⬭ *ignore*

2   Both the children in "A Great Idea" and Maria in "The Big Day" show they care by —

⬭ doing thoughtful things for someone they love

⬭ having a party

⬭ planning all the steps to make their gift

⬭ letting everyone ignore them

3   Read the diagram to answer the question.

Anne
• Has two brothers
• Makes a calendar

• Creative
• _____

Maria
• Has a sister
• Makes address labels

Which of these words fits on the blank line?

⬭ jealous

⬭ organized

⬭ bossy

⬭ unhappy

4   What makes Maria less happy than the children in "A Good Idea"?

⬭ Maria has no idea for a gift.

⬭ Maria must plan a party all alone.

⬭ Maria feels she is being ignored.

⬭ Maria doesn't like parties.

STOP

POWER Practice

TEKS 3.22A (viii) use/understand transitions; **3.29B** follow/restate/give oral instructions involving sequence; **ELPS 2I** demonstrate listening comprehension of spoken English

Listening and Speaking

Oral Instructions You follow instructions every day in all parts of your life. Read the following instructions to your partner. Have your partner listen carefully and draw the picture on a separate sheet of paper.

- **First,** turn your paper sideways and make a large rectangle. This will be the frame for your picture.

- **Second,** draw a house in the middle of your paper.

- **Third,** add windows and a front door.

- **Next,** draw a chimney on top of your house.

- **Then** put some trees and flowers outside the house.

- **Finally,** add any other details you would like and sign your picture.

When your partner is finished, switch roles.

Restate Oral Instructions

In this activity you and a partner will take turns giving and restating oral instructions on how to play your favorite game. When giving instructions, remember to use time-order words such as *first, second, third, next, then,* and *finally.*

- **Choose one person to go first. The first person gives a simple sequence of instructions for playing a game. The partner should listen carefully.**
- **Then the listener restates the instructions in order. If needed, give a clue to help your partner remember the sequence.**
- **Switch roles.**

TEKS 3.22A (viii) use/understand transitions; 3.29B follow/restate/give oral instructions involving sequence; ELPS 2D monitor understanding of spoken language/seek clarification; 2I demonstrate listening comprehension of spoken English

Listening and Speaking

Giving Instructions In this activity, you and a partner will take turns giving oral instructions about how to make or do something. Think of something you know how to do very well and can give instructions about. Here are a few examples: how to ride a bike or a skateboard, how to draw a self-portrait, or how to make a sandwich. See the box below for tips on giving instructions.

- **Choose one person to go first. The first person begins giving instructions.**

- **Remember to use time-order words such as *first*, *second*, *third*, *next*, *then*, and *finally*.**

- **When finished, make sure your partner understood the sequence of instructions.**

- **Switch roles.**

Tips for Giving Instructions

- **Explain steps one by one and in time order.**

- **Use clear and exact words and phrases.**

- **Use numbers or time-order words.**

TEKS 3.1A(iv) decode using prefixes/suffixes; 3.4A identify meanings of prefixes/suffixes; ELPS 1C use strategic learning techniques to acquire vocabulary; 3B expand/internalize initial English vocabulary; 4A learn English sound-letter relationships/decode

Vocabulary Strategies

The suffixes –ly, –tion, –sion   A suffix is a word part added to the end of a root word. When a suffix is added, it makes a new word with a different meaning. Here are some suffixes and their meanings.

-*ly* means "like or characteristic of"

-*tion* means "the act of or the state of being"

-*sion* means "act, quality, condition, or result of"

Work with a partner and write these words on cards:

act	collect	discuss	correct
careful	quick	loud	progress

Give half of the cards to your partner. On the blank side of each card, add one of the suffixes from above to make a new word. Then discuss with your partner how the suffixes change the meanings of the root words.

TEKS **3.1A(iv)** decode using prefixes/suffixes; **3.4A** identify meanings of prefixes/suffixes; **ELPS** **1C** use strategic learning techniques to acquire vocabulary; **3B** expand/internalize initial English vocabulary; **4A** learn English sound-letter relationships/decode

Word Hunt

Reread this week's selection, *The Albertosaurus Mystery.* In the story find a few examples of each of these:

- **a root word with a prefix**
- **a root word with a suffix**

Write the words you find on a separate sheet of paper. Identify the meanings of the prefixes and suffixes to help you write definitions for each word. Use your dictionary for help. Then share your words with a partner by using each word in a sentence.

TEKS **3.11** read independently/paraphrase; **3.20C** write responses to texts that demonstrate understanding; **ELPS** **4H** read silently with increasing ease/comprehension; **4I** employ reading skills to demonstrate comprehension

Independent Reading

Choose a book   When you choose a book, you may want to ask yourself the following questions.

- **Purpose**—What is my purpose, or reason, for reading? Do I want to be entertained or to learn?

- **Topic**—What topic or subject do I want to read about?

- **Genre**—Do I want to read fiction or nonfiction?

- **Difficulty**—Does this book look too easy, too difficult, or just right?

Read and Paraphrase   Once you have chosen a book, begin by reading the first chapter. At the end of your reading, paraphrase what you just read. On a separate sheet of paper, write a short paragraph. This will help you think about what you read. It will also help you remember the important parts before you start to read again.

Lesson 18

TEKS **3.3** read aloud with fluency/comprehension; **RC-3(A)** establish reading purposes; **ELPS 3H** narrate/describe/explain with detail; **4G** demonstrate comprehension through shared reading/retelling/responding/note-taking

Fluency

Partner reading With a partner, take turns reading pages from *A Tree Is Growing*. Before you read, look over the following tips for reading comprehension.

- **Set a purpose. What might be the purpose of reading a story called *A Tree Is Growing*? Do you think you will learn something new?**
- **As you read, think about what you are reading and make sure you understand it. You may have to reread a section of the text if it doesn't make sense.**
- **When you are finished reading, discuss the story with your partner. Did you learn something new about trees? Tell what you think is the most interesting thing you learned.**

335

TEKS 3.4C identify/use antonyms/synonyms/homographs/homophones; ELPS 1C use strategic learning techniques to acquire vocabulary; 1E internalize new basic/academic language

Vocabulary

Identify the Synonym A synonym is a word that means the same thing, or almost the same thing, as another word. For instance, *chilly* is a synonym for *cold*. The words listed below are from this week's story, *A Tree Is Growing*.

> giant   tiny   mixed   rough   few   cool

Each of these words is a synonym for the group of words in one of the boxes below. Select the one that best fits with each group of words. Write your answers on a separate sheet of paper.

1. large
   huge
   big
	2. coarse
	   bumpy
	   jagged
		3. combined
		   joined
		   blended

4. cold
   chilly
   frosty
	5. small
	   miniature
	   little
		6. not many
		   only some
		   hardly any

TEKS 3.1A(iv) decode using prefixes/suffixes; **3.4A** identify meanings of prefixes/suffixes; **ELPS 1C** use strategic learning techniques to acquire vocabulary; **1E** internalize new basic/academic language; **4A** learn English sound-letter relationships/decode

Vocabulary Strategies

The prefixes *pre-*, *re-*, and *bi-* A prefix is a word part that is added to the beginning of a word. Adding a prefix usually changes a word's meaning. Read the list of words below. Select one of the prefixes from the box to add to each root word. Each prefix will be used twice. Write the new words on a separate sheet of paper.

> *pre-*   *re-*   *bi-*

1. mature
2. monthly
3. historic

4. do
5. plane
6. gain

re-
pre-   bi-

Word Meaning

Remember that the prefix *re-* means "before," *re-* means "back or again," and *bi-* means "two." Adding one of these prefixes changes a root word's meaning. Copy the following chart onto a sheet of paper. Fill in each word's meaning. You may use a dictionary for help.

Word	Word's Meaning
prepare	
review	
bicycle	
revive	
bisect	
preview	

TEKS **3.16A** understand communication changes in media genres; **3.30** speak coherently/effectively about topics; **3.31** participate in discussions/build on others' ideas; **ELPS** **3G** express opinions/ideas/feelings; **3J** respond orally to information in media

Media Literacy

Compare Forms of Communication Imagine you are watching the latest space shuttle launch on television. You see the pictures of the launch and hear the sounds it makes. Now imagine you have just read a newspaper article on the same space shuttle launch. How would it be different?

The way a story is communicated on television is much different from the way it is communicated in a newspaper. This chart shows a few of the differences.

Reading a Newspaper Article	Watching a Television News Program
Printed words tell the story.	Images, sounds, and motion tell the story.
Words describe the characters, the setting and what happened. Readers use the words to create pictures in their minds.	We see the people, the setting, and what happened.

- Discuss what you know about news articles in newspapers and television news programs. Say which you prefer, and why.

TEKS **3.16A** understand communication changes in media genres; **3.30** speak coherently/effectively about topics; **3.31** participate in discussions/build on others' ideas; **ELPS** **3G** express opinions/ideas/feelings; **3J** respond orally to information in media

Make a Comparison

Copy the following chart onto a separate sheet of paper. Work with a partner and think about a recent story in the news. Did you see it on television or read about it in a newspaper? Talk with your partner about how the story might be communicated differently in each type of media. Then make a list of things that might be the same and different in the two versions of the same story.

Things That Are the Same	Things That Are Different

339

TEKS **3.16C** compare digital media written conventions; **3.19** write about personal experiences; **ELPS** **1G** distinguish between formal/informal English; **5G** narrate/describe/explain in writing

Media Literacy

Compare a News Article and an E-mail   A news article on the Internet and an informal e-mail are written in different ways. A news article usually answers the questions *who, what, when, where* and *why.* An e-mail may not give as many details.

Work with a partner on this activity. First, choose a topic to write about. Here are a few ideas:

- **something fun you did on the weekend**

- **a movie or book review**

- **a trip to the local park or zoo**

Now follow these steps:

1. **Decide if you are going to write a news article or an e-mail.**

2. **Choose your audience. Write your news article or e-mail.**

3. **When finished, exchange papers with your partner.**

4. **Talk with your partner about how the writing would be different if you had chosen the other form of writing or a different audience.**

TEKS 3.4E alphabetize to third letter/use dictionary/glossary; **ELPS** 1C use strategic learning techniques to acquire vocabulary;
1H develop/expand learning strategies; 3A practice sounds/pronunciation of English words

Vocabulary Strategies

Dictionary Fun   A dictionary gives many kinds of useful information about words. You can use a dictionary to find out what a word means, how it is divided into syllables, and how a word is pronounced.

Work with a partner. Copy this chart onto a separate sheet of paper. Take turns trying to read each word aloud. Then use a dictionary to fill in the meaning, syllabication, and pronunciation of each word listed.

Word	Meaning	Syllabication	Pronunciation
megaphone			
hazardous			
crustacean			
rhinoceros			
stalemate			
windsurfing			

Dictionary

TEKS **3.1D** identify/read contractions; **RC-3(A)** establish reading purposes; **ELPS 4C** develop/comprehend basic English vocabulary and structures

Grammar

Contractions   A contraction is two or more words shortened into one. When you make a contraction, you drop a letter or letters and use an apostrophe instead. Copy the list of contractions onto a separate sheet of paper. Then write the words that make up each contraction.

1. they're	2. aren't
3. I'm	4. he'll
5. can't	6. she's

Find Contractions

Reread *Life on the Ice*. Find the contractions used in the story. Also look for two words that can be made into a contraction. Write the words on a separate sheet of paper.

TEKS 3.1A(i) decode by dropping final "e"/adding endings; **ELPS** 4C develop/comprehend basic English vocabulary and structures

Phonics

Dropping Final e When a base word has a final *e*, the *e* must be dropped before adding the *–ed* or *–ing* ending. Look at these words:

bake   baked   baking

Write these words on a sheet of paper. Then write them again, adding the endings *–ed* and *–ing*. Read your new words out loud to a partner, and say how each is spelled.

1. dare
2. bike
3. smile

4. taste
5. care
6. vote

Word Sort

Read the words in the box.

spell	raise	correct	like	crawl
fake	sneak	skate	dare	trade

Make a chart with two columns on a separate sheet of paper. In one column, write all of the words that end with *e*. In the other column, write all of the words that don't end with *e*. Notice what happens to the spelling of each base word when you add *–ed* and *–ing* to it.

343

Lesson
21

TEKS 3.1A(ii) decode by doubling final consonants/adding endings; 3.24B(i) spell by doubling consonant before ending; **ELPS** 4C develop/comprehend basic English vocabulary and structures

Phonics

Doubling Final Consonant   Look at these words:

stop   stopped   stopping

The word *stop* is an example of a CVC (consonant, vowel, consonant) word. When the ending *–ed* or *–ing* is added to CVC words, the final consonant is doubled. Copy this chart onto a sheet of paper and fill in the blanks. The first one has been done for you. Then read each row of words on your chart out loud to a partner.

Root Word	add *-ed*	add *-ing*
tap	tapped	tapping
grab		
tan		
map		
hop		
skid		

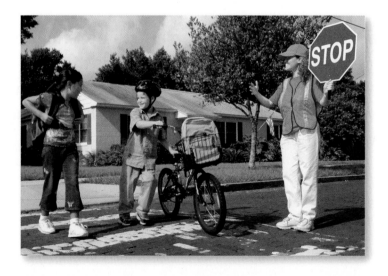

344

TEKS 3.1A(ii) decode by doubling final consonants/adding endings; **3.24B(i)** spell by doubling consonant before ending;
ELPS 4C develop/comprehend basic English vocabulary and structures

Phonics

Which Words Double Up?

Each word in the box has a base word and an ending.
Read the list out loud to a partner. Identify the base word
in each. Say which ending was added to it.

landed	snapping	dared	ripped
starring	holding	chopped	lasted

Now copy the chart below. Write each base word under
the heading that tells what happens to its spelling when
–*ed* or –*ing* is added to it.

Doubles Final Consonant	Does Not Double Final Consonant

TEKS **3.1A(iii)** decode by changing final "y" to "i"; **3.24B(iii)** spell by changing "y" to "i" before ending; **RC-3(A)** establish reading purposes; **ELPS** **4C** develop/comprehend basic English vocabulary and structures

Phonics

Changing Final *y* to *i*   When you add endings such as *–ed* and *–es* to words that end in *y*, you sometimes have to change the *y* to *i* before adding the ending. Look at the following example:

story   stories

Work with a partner to make word cards.

- On one side of a card, write a word that needs to have the final *y* changed to *i* before adding the ending *–ed* or *–es*. Repeat until you have five word cards.

- Switch cards with your partner.

- Look at the word cards from your partner. Add *–ed* or *–es* to each word and write the new word on the back side of the card.

- Take turn reading both sets of word cards out loud.

Find *y* to *i* Words

Reread this week's selection, *The Journey: Stories of Migration*. In the selection find some examples of each of these things:

- root words that end in *y* and need to have the final *y* changed to *i* before adding an *–ed* or *–es* ending.
- words that end in *–ed* or *–es*. Did the root word end in *y* before the *–ed* or *–es* ending was added?

Write the words you find on a sheet of paper. Read your list to a partner. Then swap lists and read each other's words.

TEKS 3.1A(iii) decode by changing final "y" to "i"; **3.24B(iii)** spell by changing "y" to "i" before ending; **ELPS 4C** develop/comprehend basic English vocabulary and structures

Phonics

Make New Words   You learned that when you add endings such as *–ed* and *–es* to words that end in *y*, you sometimes have to change the *y* to *i* before adding the ending. Copy this chart. Add the endings *–ed* and *–es* to each word to complete it. Remember to change the *y* to *i* when necessary. Read the new words.

Root Word	add *-ed* ending	add *-ing* ending
rely		
worry		
carry		
hurry		
try		

What Is the Root Word?

Read the words in the box. In the root of each word, the final *y* changed to *i* before the ending was added. Identify each root word and write it on a separate sheet of paper.

hurries	pried	flies
applied	married	worries

TEKS **3.1A(i)** decode by dropping final "e"/adding endings; **3.24B(ii)** spell by dropping final "e" before ending; **ELPS** **4A** learn English sound-letter relationships/decode; **4C** develop/comprehend basic English vocabulary and structures

Phonics

Dropping Final e When a base word has a final e, the e must be dropped before adding the –ed or –ing ending. Look at the words in green. Notice that the e was dropped before the endings were added.

stare   stared   staring

Copy this chart. Then fill in the blank spaces. Once your chart is complete, read across each row, tapping words that have spelling changes when endings are added.

Root Word	–ed ending	–ing ending
fake	faked	faking
chase		
	shined	
		confiding
	danced	
bake		
		bruising

The Final e Challenge

Play this game with a partner.

- **Write ten words on a separate sheet of paper. Write some words that end in an e and some that do not.**
- **Switch papers with your partner.**
- **Find the words that need the final e dropped before adding the –ed and –ing endings. Circle these words.**
- **Write the new words with the –ed and –ing endings.**

TEKS 3.1A(ii) decode by doubling final consonants/adding endings; 3.24B(i) spell by doubling consonant before ending; **ELPS** 4A learn English sound-letter relationships/decode; 4C develop/comprehend basic English vocabulary and structures

Phonics

Doubling Final Consonants   The word *slap* is an example of a CVC (consonant, vowel, consonant) word. When the ending *–ed* or *–ing* is added to CVC words, the final consonant is doubled.

slap   slapped   slapping

Copy the words below. Then make new words by adding the endings *–ed* and *–ing* to them. Compare your final list of words with a partner's, noticing any spelling changes. Take turns reading your lists aloud.

1. **ram**
2. **clip**
3. **infer**
4. **bug**
5. **can**
6. **rob**

Find the Word

Read each sentence below. Each underlined word below needs its final consonant doubled and an *–ed* or *–ing* ending added. Write the correct form of each word on a separate sheet of paper.

1. **Max <u>beg</u> his dad to let him keep the puppy.**
2. **Please stop <u>drag</u> your backpack on the ground.**
3. **The parents want to keep <u>chat</u> all night long.**
4. **Joe started <u>mop</u> the floor.**
5. **After the race, the winner <u>pin</u> the blue ribbon on her shirt.**

TEKS **3.1A(iv)** decode using prefixes/suffixes; **3.4A** identify meanings of prefixes/suffixes; **ELPS 4A** learn English sound-letter relationships/ decode; **4C** develop/comprehend basic English vocabulary and structures

Vocabulary Strategies

Prefix or Suffix? A prefix is a word part that is added to the beginning of a word. A suffix is a word part that is added to the end of a word. Read each word in the box below. Decide if it has a prefix or a suffix. Then copy the chart. Write each word in the correct column.

import	joyful	harmless	unsafe
resend	inside	shameful	imperfect
careless	inspire	wonderful	thankless

Words with Prefixes	Words with Suffixes

Prefix and Suffix Word Cards

Remember that adding prefixes and suffixes to words often changes the meaning of the root word. Work with a partner to make prefix and suffix word cards.

- Reread this week's selection, *The Journey: Stories of Migration*.
- Find story words that have prefixes and suffixes and write them on word cards.
- Switch cards with your partner.
- On the back of each word card, write the meaning of the word.
- Discuss with your partner how the prefixes or suffixes changed the meanings of the root words.

TEKS 3.1A(iv) decode using prefixes/suffixes; 3.4A identify meanings of prefixes/suffixes; ELPS 4A learn English sound-letter relationships/ decode; 4C develop/comprehend basic English vocabulary and structures

Vocabulary Strategies

The Suffixes –er, –est A suffix is a word part added to the end of a root word. When you add a suffix, you make a new word with a different meaning. The suffix *–er* means "more" or "one who." The suffix *–est* means "most." Read these words, then copy them on a separate sheet of paper. After each word, write the root word.

1. colder
2. fastest
3. shiniest
4. rounder
5. redder
6. happiest

New Word Meanings

Copy the chart below on a sheet of paper, then complete it. Then compare your chart with a partner's, discussing any differences. Take turns reading each row.

Root Word	Suffix	New Word	New Meaning
sharp	-er	sharper	more sharp
sharp	-est		
great	-er		
great	-est		
nice	-er		
nice	-est		
young	-er		

TEKS 3.16A understand communication changes in media genres; **ELPS** 1A use prior knowledge/experiences; 5G narrate/describe/explain in writing

Media Literacy

Radio, Newspaper, and Television   Think about the differences between these three communication sources: radio, newspaper, and television. When you listen to a radio, do you see any pictures? No, you only hear words. You may create pictures in your mind of what is being said. Articles in a newspaper also use words to tell a story. Readers use the words to create pictures in their minds, too. Television uses images and sounds as well as words to tell a story. We see and hear what is happening.

Make a Comparison

Work with a partner on this activity. Imagine that you want to find out what happened in yesterday's baseball game. You have three choices: you can listen to a radio sports report, read the newspaper, or watch the news on television. Which would you choose? Why?

Copy the chart on a separate sheet of paper. Tell how the news would be communicated differently on the radio, in the newspaper, and on television.

Radio	Newspaper	Television

TEKS **3.16C** compare digital media written conventions; ELPS **1G** distinguish between formal/informal media; **5C** spell English words with increasing accuracy; **5D** edit writing for standard grammar/usage

Media Literacy

Write an E-mail E-mail is a popular form of communication. Writing an e-mail is different from other kinds of written communication. In this activity you are going to practice writing an e-mail.

- Work with a partner.

- Follow the guidelines in the box below when writing your e-mail.

- Write an e-mail to your partner telling about something fun you did last weekend or recently. Have your partner do the same.

- When you finish, trade and read each other's e-mails.

- Discuss with your partner how your writing would be different if you were asked to write a news article or some other form of written communication.

Guidelines for Writing E-mail

1. Give your message a specific title in the subject line.

2. Use short paragraphs. Long paragraphs are difficult to read onscreen.

3. Skip a line instead of indenting when you begin a new paragraph.

4. Remember that special type, such as italics or underlining, may not show up on the other person's screen.

5. Even though an e-mail may seem more casual than a letter, you should still follow the rules of good writing.

6. Proofread your e-mail, and fix all capitalization, punctuation, usage, and spelling mistakes.

TEKS **3.1E** monitor decoding accuracy; **ELPS** **4A** learn English sound-letter relationships/decode; **4H** read silently with increasing ease/comprehension

Phonics

Decoding Unfamiliar Words   Read this article. As you read, pause to decode unfamiliar words. First, look for context clues in the rest of the sentence or in sentences around it. Next, look for familiar word parts, such as prefixes or suffixes. Last, divide the word into syllables, or smaller word parts, that you can pronounce.

Birth of a Butterfly

Soon after a butterfly lays her eggs, baby caterpillars hatch. Most caterpillars have multiple eyes, but they can only sense light and dark. The caterpillar has a head and thirteen body segments. It has eight pairs of legs. The first three pairs of legs will become the butterfly's legs.

The caterpillar eats and eats until it gets very big. Then it climbs on a leaf or twig and creates a shell called a cocoon. Inside the cocoon, a transformation takes place.

When the cocoon opens, a butterfly appears. Butterflies have six legs and two sets of wings. They are great flyers. Some butterflies, like the Monarch, have a maximum speed of up to 20 miles per hour.

Work with a partner on this activity.

- **Take turns reading the paragraphs aloud with a partner.**
- **List words that were difficult for you.**
- **Compare your list with your partner's. Tell how you decoded each word.**

TEKS **3.1A(iv)** decode using prefixes/suffixes; **3.4A** identify meanings of prefixes/suffixes; **ELPS** **4A** learn English sound-letter relationships/ decode; **4C** develop/comprehend basic English vocabulary and structures

Vocabulary Strategies

re-

pre-

un-

bi-

Prefix and Root Match   You have learned that a prefix is a word part that is added to the beginning of a word. Adding a prefix usually changes a word's meaning.

Look at the words in the boxes. One box contains prefixes, and the other contains root words. Combine a prefix and a root word to make new words. Some prefixes may be used with more than one of the root words. Write the new words on a separate sheet of paper.

Prefixes
un-
pre-
re-
bi-

Root Words	
told	cook
fill	mind
roll	pay
cycle	view

Prefix Word Cards

Look at the meanings of these prefixes:

un- means "not"   *pre-* means "before"

re- means "back or again"   *bi-* means "two"

Work with a partner to create prefix word cards.

• Write a word on a card that can have one of the prefixes from the list above added to it. Repeat until you have five word cards.

• Switch cards with a partner. Add a prefix and write the new word and its meaning on the back of the card.

• Take turns reading the words on the word cards aloud.

TEKS 3.1A(iv) decode using prefixes/suffixes; **3.4A** identify meanings of prefixes/suffixes; **ELPS** 4A learn English sound-letter relationships/decode; **4C** develop/comprehend basic English vocabulary and structures

Vocabulary Strategies

Remove the Suffix Suffixes are word parts that are added to the end of words. When you add a suffix to a root word, the word's meaning usually changes. You also may need to drop or change a letter from the root word when you add a suffix. Copy the list of words onto a separate sheet of paper. Remove the suffix from each word and write the root word.

1. careless

2. valuable

3. happiness

4. comfortable

5. colorless

6. goodness

What Does It Mean?

Read the suffixes and their meanings.

-less means "without"

-ness means "quality or state"

-able means "capable of"

Copy the following words. Add one of the suffixes to each word. Then write the meaning of the new word.

1. wash

2. kind

3. sleep

4. rely

5. help

6. rough

Glossary

This glossary contains meanings and pronunciations for some of the words in this book. The Full Pronunciation Key shows how to pronounce each consonant and vowel in a special spelling. At the bottom of the glossary pages is a shortened form of the full key.

Full Pronunciation Key

Consonant Sounds

b	**bib**, ca**bb**age	kw	**ch**oir, **qu**ick	t	**t**igh**t**, stopp**ed**
ch	**ch**ur**ch**, sti**tch**	l	**l**id, need**le**, ta**ll**	th	ba**th**, **th**in
d	**d**ee**d**, mail**ed**, pu**dd**le	m	a**m**, **m**an, du**mb**	*th*	ba**th**e, **th**is
		n	**n**o, sudde**n**	v	ca**v**e, val**v**e, **v**ine
f	**f**ast, **f**i**f**e, o**ff**, **ph**rase, rou**gh**	ng	thi**ng**, i**nk**	w	**w**ith, **w**olf
g	**g**a**g**, **g**et, fin**g**er	p	**p**o**p**, ha**pp**y	y	**y**es, **y**olk, on**i**on
h	**h**at, **wh**o	r	**r**oar, **rh**yme	z	ro**s**e, si**z**e, **x**ylophone, **z**ebra
hw	**wh**ich, **wh**ere	s	mi**ss**, **s**au**c**e, **sc**ene, **s**ee	zh	gara**g**e, plea**s**ure, vi**s**ion
j	**j**ud**g**e, **g**em	sh	di**sh**, **sh**ip, **s**ugar, ti**ss**ue		
k	**c**at, **k**ick, s**ch**ool				

Vowel Sounds

ă	p**a**t, l**au**gh	ŏ	h**o**rrible, p**o**t	ŭ	c**u**t, fl**oo**d, r**ou**gh, s**o**me
ā	**a**pe, **ai**d, p**ay**	ō	g**o**, r**ow**, t**oe**, th**ough**	û	c**i**rcle, f**u**r, h**ea**rd, t**e**rm, t**u**rn, **u**rge, w**o**rd
â	**ai**r, c**a**re, w**ea**r	ô	**a**ll, c**au**ght, f**o**r, p**aw**		
ä	f**a**ther, k**oa**la, y**a**rd	oi	b**oy**, n**oi**se, **oi**l		
ĕ	p**e**t, pl**ea**sure, **a**ny	ou	c**ow**, **ou**t	yo͝o	c**u**re
ē	b**e**, b**ee**, **ea**sy, pian**o**	o͝o	f**u**ll, b**oo**k, w**o**lf	yo͞o	ab**u**se, **u**se
ĭ	**i**f, p**i**t, b**u**sy	o͞o	b**oo**t, r**u**de, fr**ui**t, fl**ew**	ə	**a**go, sil**e**nt, penc**i**l, lem**o**n, circ**u**s
ī	r**i**de, b**y**, p**ie**, h**igh**				
î	d**ea**r, d**ee**r, f**ie**rce, m**e**re				

Stress Marks

Primary Stress ´: bi·ol·o·gy [bī ŏl´ ə jē]
Secondary Stress ´: bi·o·log·i·cal [bī´ ə lŏj´ ĭ kəl]

A

a·board (ə **bôrd´**) *adverb and preposition* On, onto, or inside a vehicle, such as a ship, train, or bus: *The captain welcomed us aboard as we stepped onto the ship's deck.*

ab·sorb (əb **sôrb´**) *verb* Take in or soak up: *A sponge can absorb lots of water.*

ac·ci·dent (**ăk´** sĭ dənt) *noun* An event that is not expected and not wanted: *Traffic was held up by two accidents on the highway.*

al·ti·tude (**ăl´** tĭ tōōd´) *noun* A height measured from sea level or from the earth's surface: *The plane flew at an altitude of 30,000 feet.*

an·chor (**ăng´** kər) *noun* A heavy metal object, attached to a ship, that is dropped overboard to keep the ship in place: *It took two sailors to raise the heavy anchor when the ship was ready to sail.*

an·cient (**ān´** shənt) *adjective* Very old; having existed for a long time: *They discovered an ancient treasure.*

an·nu·al (**ăn´** yōō əl) *adjective* Happening every year: *The annual town picnic is next week.*

ap·proach (ə **prōch´**) *verb* To come near or nearer: *As the storm approached, people were told to leave their seaside homes.*

ar·riv·al (ə **rī´** vəl) *noun* The act of reaching a place: *We waited for the arrival of our guests.*

av·a·lanche (**ăv´** ə lănch´) *noun* A large amount of snow, ice, or earth that falls down a mountain: *Skiers should be warned of the danger of avalanches on this mountain.*

B

base (bās) *noun* The lowest part; bottom: *We camped at the base of the cliff.*

bay (bā) *noun* A part of the sea that cuts into the land: *Have you ever seen sharks swimming in this bay?*

bur·y (**bĕr´** ē) *verb* Cover from view; hide: *I buried my face in the pillow.*

C

car·ton (**kär´** tn) *noun* A cardboard box used to hold goods: *Let's pack these gifts into a mailing carton.*

carton

ă r**a**t / ā p**ay** / â c**are** / ä f**a**ther / ĕ p**e**t / ē b**e** / ĭ p**i**t / ī p**ie** / î f**ie**rce / ŏ p**o**t / ō g**o** / ô p**aw**, f**or** / oi **oi**l / ōō b**oo**k

chill·y (chĭl´ ē) *adjective* Unpleasantly cold: *Please take a jacket if the weather is damp and chilly.*

cli·mate (klī´ mĭt) *noun* The usual weather that occurs in a place: *The climate in polar areas is very harsh.*

clue (klo͞o) *noun* Something that helps to solve a problem or mystery: *Here are some more clues to the riddle.*

clump (klŭmp) *noun* Thick cluster or group: *Watch out for clumps of poison ivy along the path!*

col·o·ny (kŏl´ ə nē) *noun* A group of living things of the same kind living or growing together: *A colony of bees built a hive in the tree.*

com·pli·ca·ted (kŏm´ plĭ kā´ tĭd) *adjective* Not easy to understand, deal with, or solve: *Did you do the complicated problem on page 5?*

con·stant (kŏn´ stənt) *adjective* Without a break or pause: *The car is in constant use.*

con·ver·sa·tion (kŏn´ vər sā´ shən) *noun* Informal talk between two or more people: *My sister has some long phone conversations with her friends.*

cov·er·ing (kŭv´ ər ĭng) *noun* Something that covers: *If it rains during our camping trip, we can put waterproof coverings on the tents.*

cur·rent·ly (kûr´ ənt lē) *adverb* At the present time; now: *That movie is currently showing.*

D

depth (dĕpth) *noun* Distance from top to bottom or front to back: *Crater Lake, with a depth of over 1,900 feet, is our deepest lake.*

des·ert (dĕz´ ərt) *noun* A dry area, usually covered with sand, in which few plants or animals live: *Animals that can get by with little water often live in deserts.*

dis·solve (dĭ zŏlv´) *verb* To change from a solid to a liquid: *To make hot chocolate, dissolve sugar and cocoa powder in hot milk*

dra·mat·ic (drə măt´ ĭk) *adjective* Exciting: *The dramatic ending of the play left the audience stunned.*

drip (drĭp) *verb* To fall or let fall in drops: *Water is dripping into the attic from a leak in the roof.*

E

e·mer·gen·cy (ĭ mûr´ jən sē) *adjective* Giving urgent, immediate action or care: *The emergency animal hospital is open all night.*

clue
Clue is sometimes spelled *clew*. In a Greek myth, a prince named Theseus was jailed by King Minos. To escape, Theseus had to enter a maze, battle a creature called the Minotaur, and find his way out of the maze again. Theseus used a clew, a ball of thread, to guide him out of the maze.

drip

e·quip·ment (ĭ kwĭp´ mənt) *noun* The things that are needed for a purpose: *This store sells camping equipment.*

ev·i·dence (ĕv´ ĭ dəns) *noun* Facts or signs that help one find out the truth or decide: *The broken window was evidence that a burglary had taken place.*

ex·treme (ĭk strēm´) *adjective* Very great: *The Arctic explorers suffered from the extreme cold.*

fiery

F

fierce (fîrs) *adjective* Wild and savage; dangerous: *Tigers can be fierce animals.*

fier·y (fīr´ ē) *adjective* Of or glowing like fire: *The fiery red and orange sunset was beautiful.*

fos·sil (fŏs´ əl) *noun* The remains or traces of a plant or animal of an earlier age: *These tiny fossils are the bones of ancient birds.*

fright·en·ing (frīt´ nĭng) *adjective* Scary: *We spent a frightening few minutes listening to the bear outside our tent.*

G

glass·y (glăs´ ē) *adjective* Smooth, clear, and shiny; like glass: *We skated on the glassy surface of the frozen pond.*

glide (glīd) *verb* To move smoothly, quietly, and with ease: *Many skaters were gliding gracefully around the ice rink.*

glob·al (glō´ bəl) *adjective* Worldwide; relating to the entire earth: *Many countries are cooperating in a global effort to end hunger.*

guide (gīd) *verb* To show the way to; direct: *The ranger guided us along the park's trails.*

H

halt (hôlt) *verb* To come or bring to a stop: *Police will halt traffic to let the parade pass.*

hard·ly (härd´ lē) *adverb* Barely; only just: *This box is so heavy I can hardly lift it.*

hor·ri·fy·ing (hôr´ ə fī´ ĭng) *adjective* Causing strong fear or horror: *Some nightmares can be truly horrifying.*

ă rat / ā pay / â care / ä father / ě pet / ē be / ĭ pit / ī pie / î fierce / ŏ pot / ō go / ô paw, for / oi oil / ŏŏ book

I

im·me·di·ate·ly (ĭ mē′ dē ĭt lē)
adverb At once; right away:
*If you hear an alarm, leave the
building **immediately**.*

in·crease (ĭn **krēs′**) *verb* To
make or become greater
or larger: *As your height
increases, you usually gain
weight, too.*

in·spire (ĭn **spīr′**) *verb* To
move to action: *The promise
of money **inspired** me to work
hard.*

L

land·scape (**lănd′** skāp′)
noun A stretch of land that
is viewed as scenery: *We
watched the desert **landscape**
from the car window.*

la·va (**lă′** və) *noun* Melted
rock that flows from a volcano:
*Hot **lava** oozed down the side
of the volcano.*

lay·er (**lā′** ər) *noun* A single
thickness, coating, or sheet of
material covering a surface:
*Sprinkle a **layer** of cheese on
top of the tomato sauce.*

lev·el (**lĕv′** əl) *noun* A certain
height: *I waded in until the
water was at chest **level**.*

liq·uid (**lĭk′** wĭd) *noun* A
substance that flows easily:
*Pour the **liquid** slowly into the
flour and sugar mixture and stir
well.*

load (lōd) *verb* To put into
a vehicle or structure for
carrying: *The dock workers
loaded grain onto the ship.*

lo·ca·tion (lō **kā′** shən)
noun A place where
something is or can be found:
*We finally found the **location** of
the airport.*

love·ly (**lŭv′** lē) *adjective*
Beautiful; very pleasing: *Their
garden is the **loveliest** one I
have ever seen.*

loy·al (**lo** i(-ə)l)
adjective Faithful: *Shiva is a
loyal friend, and I can always
depend on him to help me.*

ly·ing (**lī** ing) *verb* Being in a
flat or resting position: *Uncle
Morris is **lying** on the couch,
taking a nap.*

M

man·age (**măn′** ĭj) *verb* To
succeed in doing something:
*I **managed** to finish my work
ahead of time.*

meas·ure (**mĕzh′** ər) *verb* To
find the size, amount, capacity,
or degree of: *Using a
yardstick, Mom **measured** how
tall we were each year.*

lava
The word *lava*
comes from an
Italian word. The
Italian word, in
turn, came from
the latin word
labes, meaning
"fall."

measure

ōo b**oo**t / ou **ou**t / ŭ c**u**t / û f**u**r / hw **wh**ich / th **th**in / *th* **th**is / zh vi**s**ion / ə
ago, sil**e**nt, penc**i**l, lem**o**n, circ**u**s

mi·grate (mī´ grāt) *verb* To move regularly from one region or climate to another: *Many birds **migrate** south in the fall.*

mys·te·ri·ous (mĭ **stîr´** ē əs) *adjective* Very hard to explain or understand: *A **mysterious** light came from the empty house.*

N

nar·row (năr´ ō) *adjective* Small or thin in width: *The road was long and **narrow**.*

O

o·ver·heat·ed (ō´ vər **hēt´** ĭd) *adjective* Too hot: *Pets can easily get **overheated** on hot summer days.*

P

pan·ick·ing (păn´ ĭk ĭng) *adjective* Having a sudden feeling of great fear: *The **panicking** crowd pushed and shoved as they ran out of the building.*

part·ner (pärt nər) *noun* Someone who work or plays with one or more others: *The two **partners** took turns making and selling their lemonade.*

pas·sage (păs ĭj) *noun* Narrow pathway or channel: *Busy ants dig a maze of **passages** in each anthill.*

pa·trol (pə **trol**) *verb* To move around an area in order to watch or guard: *Workers **patrol** the museum to make sure no one touches the paintings.*

pleas·ure (plĕzh´ ər) *noun* A feeling of happiness or enjoyment; delight: *She smiled with **pleasure** when she saw the puppies.*

plen·ty (plĕn´ tē) *noun* A full supply or amount: *Children need **plenty** of exercise.*

pol·len (pŏl´ ən) *noun* Tiny grains that fertilize female plants to produce seeds: *Flower **pollen** makes new plants grow, but it also makes me sneeze all spring!*

pol·lu·tion (pə **loo´** shən) *noun* The act of making dirty, impure, or harmful; the condition of being dirty, impure, or harmful: *Smog is a kind of air **pollution**.*

pre·his·tor·ic (prē´ hĭ **stôr´** ĭk) *adjective* Of, relating to, or belonging to the time before people began to record events in writing: *The bones of a **prehistoric** animal were found in a cave.*

ă rat / ā pay / â care / ä father / ĕ pet / ē be / ĭ pit / ī pie / î fierce / ŏ pot / ō go / ô paw, for / oi oil / ōō book

proj·ect (prŏj´ ĕkt´) *noun*
A plan for doing something;
scheme: *The town's voters
approved the building **project**.*

prove (prōov) *verb* To show
to be true by backing up with
facts: *Getting an A on the test
will **prove** that you studied.*

puz·zling (pŭz´ lĭng) *adjective*
Confusing; baffling: *I could
not put the toy together
because the directions were
so **puzzling**.*

Q

quiv·er (**kwi** vər) *verb* Shake;
tremble: *The squirrel began to
quiver with fear when my dog
got too close.*

R

re·cy·cle (rē **sī**´ kəl) *verb* To
treat materials that have
been thrown away in order
to use them again: *Many
cities **recycle** glass, cans, and
newspapers.*

re·gion (rē´ jən) *noun* A
usually large area of the earth's
surface: *This **region** receives
very little rainfall each year.*

re·mains (rĭ **mānz**´) *noun*
All or part of a dead body:
*The **remains** of this polar
bear were covered by ice for
hundreds of years.*

re·un·ion (rē **yōōn**´ yən)
noun A gathering of the
members of a group who have
been separated: *Our family
has a yearly **reunion**.*

rip·ple (**rĭp**´ əl) *verb* To form
or cause to form small waves:
*The surface of the river **rippled**
when I skipped a stone across it.*

rub·bish (**rŭb**´ ĭsh) *noun*
Trash: *Please take this
rubbish out to the trash can.*

S

sci·en·tif·ic (sī´ ən **tĭf**´ ĭk)
adjective Of, relating to, or
used in science: ***Scientific**
studies have shown that this
product works.*

scout (skout) *noun* Someone
who goes out from a group to
gather information: *The **scout**
returned to camp and told us
about the tracks he had found.*

sec·tion (**sĕk**´ shən) *noun*
A part taken from a whole:
*A slice is a **section** of a cake
or pie.*

shade (shād) *noun* An area
that is partly dark because light
has been blocked off from it:
*It is too cold to sit in the **shade**.*

shel·ter (**shĕl**´ tər) *noun*
Something that protects or
covers: *Stand under the
shelter at the bus stop if it's
raining.*

reunion
The word *reunion*
was formed
by joining the
Latin prefix *re-*,
meaning "again,"
with the Late
Latin word *unire*,
meaning "to
unite." Therefore,
reunion means
"to unite again."

section

ōō b**oo**t / ou **out** / ŭ c**u**t / û f**u**r / hw **wh**ich / th **th**in / *th* **th**is / zh vi**s**ion / ə
ago, sil**e**nt, penc**i**l, lem**o**n, circ**u**s

shift (shift) *noun* A scheduled period of work: *My brother works an early-morning shift at the restaurant.*

sin·cere (sĭn sîr´) *adjective* Honest; real; genuine: *Our feelings are sincere.*

skel·e·ton (skĕl´ ĭ tn) *noun* The framework of bones in the body of a human being or an animal having a backbone: *People training to be doctors study skeletons to learn about human bones.*

slope (slōp) *noun* A stretch of ground that slants upward or downward: *The slopes on the hills behind our house are great for sledding.*

snap (snap) *verb* To bite or try to bite with a sudden motion: *A wild animal may snap at you if you try to pet it.*

sog·gy (sô´ gē) *adjective* Soaked; very wet: *My shoe was soggy after the dog put it in the wading pool.*

sol·id (sŏl´ ĭd) *adjective* Hard: *Those swans were carved from solid ice.*

spine (spīn) *noun* Part of a plant or animal that sticks out with a sharp point: *Porcupines are covered in prickly spines, or quills.*

spot (spŏt) *verb* To see, find, or locate: *The bird watchers spotted a huge woodpecker on their walk.*

store (stôr) *verb* Put away for future use: *Squirrels store acorns for winter.*

suc·ceed (sək sēd´) *verb* To carry out something desired or tried: *We will succeed at reaching our goal if we all work together.*

sum·mit (sŭm´ ĭt) *noun* The highest point or part; top: *We rode a ski lift to the summit of the mountain and then zoomed down.*

sur·round (sə round´) *verb* To be on all sides of; encircle: *The people of the village built a wall that surrounded the whole town.*

sur·viv·al (sər vī´ vəl) *noun* The act or fact of staying alive: *The family's survival is due to the firefighters' quick action.*

T

tank (tăngk) *noun* A container for holding or storing liquids or gases: *Divers always check to be sure that their tanks are filled with air.*

tem·per·a·ture (tĕm´ pər ə chər) *noun* Hotness or coldness as measured on a standard scale: *The temperature is warmer in the sun than in the shade.*

ter·ror (tĕr´ ər) *noun* Very great fear: *I screamed in terror as the roller coaster turned upside down.*

ă rat / ā pay / â care / ä father / ĕ pet / ē be / ĭ pit / ī pie / î fierce / ŏ pot / ō go / ô paw, for / oi oil / o͞o book

through·out (thrōō **out´**)
preposition In, to, or through
every part of: *We walked
throughout the city and saw all
the sights.*

thun·der·ous (**thŭn´** dər əs)
adjective Loud and rumbling:
*A thunderous noise woke
everyone up.*

trench (trĕnch) *noun* A long,
narrow ditch: *The workers
dug a trench and then laid
pipes in it.*

trop·i·cal (**trŏp´** ĭ kəl)
adjective From or typical of
the tropics, the warm areas
of Earth near the equator:
*Mangoes and bananas are
both tropical fruits.*

twist (twĭst) *verb* To wind
together to form a single
strand: *I watched as the
woman twisted her long hair
into a beautiful braid.*

U

un·a·ware (ŭn´ ə **wâr´**)
adjective Without knowledge
of: *They were unaware that
their actions were being
recorded.*

un·cov·er (ŭn **kŭv´** ər)
verb To reveal or remove the
cover from: *Workers digging
the tunnels are uncovering
many objects from an earlier
time.*

un·der·ground
(**ŭn´** dər ground´)
adjective Located below the
surface of the ground: *An
underground passage connects
the two buildings.*

un·ex·pect·ed (ŭn´ ĭk **spĕk´** tĭd)
adjective Taking place without
warning: *We gasped when we
heard the unexpected news.*

V

vi·o·lent·ly (**vī´** ə lənt lē)
adverb With great physical
force: *Waves crashed violently
against the cliffs during the
storm.*

voy·age (**voi´** ĭj) *noun* A
long journey made on a ship,
aircraft, or spacecraft: *The
astronauts will remember their
voyage to the moon for the rest
of their lives.*

W

wil·der·ness (**wĭl´** dər nĭs)
noun An area in a wild,
natural state in which there
are no people: *You might see
unusual animals and plants in
a wilderness.*

with·in (wĭth **ĭn´**) *preposition*
Not going beyond the limits
of: *We'll learn the results of
the test within the next few
days.*

underground

Underground is a
compound word, or
a word made from
two or more shorter
words. Compound
words can be
spelled as one word
(*underground*), as
two words (*air mail*),
or as two words
joined by a hyphen
(*hard-boiled*).

ōō b**oo**t / ou **ou**t / ŭ **cu**t / û f**u**r / hw **wh**ich / th **th**in / *th* **th**is / zh vi**si**on / ə
ago, sil**e**nt, penc**i**l, lem**o**n, circ**u**s

Acknowledgments

Main Literature Selections

The Albertosaurus Mystery: Philip Currie's Hunt in the Badlands by T. V. Padma. Copyright © 2007 by Bearport Publishing Company, Inc. All rights reserved. Reprinted by permission with Bearport Publishing Company, Inc.

"The Army Ants" from *Insectlopedia* by Douglas Florian. Copyright © 1998 by Douglas Florian. Reprinted by permission of Houghton Mifflin Harcourt Publishing Company.

Dog-of-the-Sea-Waves written and illustrated by James Rumford. Copyright © 2004 by James Rumford. All rights reserved. Reprinted by permission of Houghton Mifflin Harcourt Publishing Company.

Dogzilla by Dav Pilkey. Copyright © 1995 by Dav Pilkey. All rights reserved. Reprinted by permission of Houghton Mifflin Harcourt Publishing Company.

The Journey of Oliver K. Woodman by Darcy Pattison, illustrated by Joe Cepeda. Text copyright © 2003 by Darcy Pattison. Illustrations copyright © 2003 by Joe Cepeda. Reprinted by permission of Houghton Mifflin Harcourt Publishing Company.

The Journey: Stories of Migration written by Cynthia Rylant. Text copyright © 2006 by Cynthia Rylant. Reprinted by permission of The Blue Sky Press, a division of Scholastic, Inc.

"Knockabout and Knockaboom" from *A World of Wonders: Geographic Travels in Verse and Rhyme* by J. Patrick Lewis. Copyright © 2002 by J. Patrick Lewis. Reprinted by permission of Dial Books for Young Readers, A Division of Penguin Young Readers Group, A Member of Penguin Group (USA) Inc., 345 Hudson Street, New York, NY 10014, and Curtis Brown, Ltd.

Life on the Ice by Susan E. Goodman with photographs by Michael J. Doolittle. Text copyright © 2006 by Susan E. Goodman. Photographs copyright © 2006 by Michael J. Doolittle, except where noted. Reprinted by permission of Millbrook Press, a division of Lerner Publishing Group, Inc. All rights reserved.

"Mountain Mist/Neible del monte" from *From the Bellybutton of the Moon and Other Summer Poems/ Del ombligo de la luna y otras poemas de verano* by Francisco X. Alarcón. Copyright © 1998 by Francisco X. Alarcón. Reprinted by permission of the publisher, Children's Book Press, San Francisco, CA, www.childrensbookpress.org.

Mountains: Surviving Mt. Everest by Michael Sandler. Copyright © 2006 by Bearport Publishing Company, Inc. All rights reserved. Reprinted by permission of Bearport Publishing Company, Inc.

"A Mr. Rubbish Mood" from *Judy Moody Saves the World!* by Megan McDonald, illustrated by Peter H. Reynolds. Text copyright © 2002 by Megan McDonald, Illustrations copyright © 2002 by Peter H. Reynolds. Reprinted by permission of the publisher, Candlewick Press, Inc., and the author.

A Tree is Growing by Arthur Dorros, illustrated by S.D. Schindler. Text copyright © 1997 by Arthur Dorros. Illustrations copyright © 1997 by S.D. Schindler. Reprinted by permission of Scholastic Press, a division of Scholastic, Inc.

Two Bad Ants written and illustrated by Chris Van Allsburg. Copyright © 1988 by Chris Van Allsburg. All rights reserved. Reprinted by permission of Houghton Mifflin Harcourt Publishing Company.

"Until I Saw the Sea" from *I Feel the Same Way* by Lilian Moore. Copyright © 1967 by Lilian Moore. Reprinted by permission of the author c/o Marian Reiner, Literary Agent.

"Upside Down" from *When It Comes to Bugs* by Aileen Fisher. Copyright © 1986 Aileen Fisher. Reprinted by permission of the Boulder Public Library Foundation, Inc., c/o Marian Reiner, Literary Agent.

Credits

Photo Credits

Placement Key: (t) top; (b) bottom; (l) left; (r) right; (c) center; (bg) background; (fg) foreground; (i) inset.

TOC 4 t (c) Kevin Schafer/Corbis; **TOC 4** bkgd t age fotostock/SuperStock; **TOC 4** c (c) Jonathan Blair/CORBIS; **TOC 4** b Michael & Patricia Fogden/Minden Pictures; **TOC 5** t Photodisc/SuperStock; **TOC 5** c AP Photo/Sun-Times, Scott Stewart; **TOC 6** t WildPictures/Alamy; **TOC 6** b Getty Images/blue jean images RF; **TOC 7** t (c) Stapleton Collection/Corbis; **TOC 7** c Stuart Westmorland/Getty Images; **9** c (c) Brandon D. Cole/CORBIS; **10** cl Thinkstock Images/Jupiter Images; **10** cr (c) Getty Images; **10** bl Digital Vision/Getty Images; **10** br (c) Tom Grill/Corbis; **10** t (c) Kevin Schafer/CORBIS; **10** bkgd t age fotostock/SuperStock; **11** tl (c) Javier Larrea/age fotostock; **11** tc Paul Hurst/Alamy; **11** tr Stockbyte/Getty Images; **11** bl Bob Elam/Alamy; **11** bc Barry Mason/Alamy; **11** br (c) G. Baden/zefa/Corbis; **14** t Courtesy Candlewick Press; **14** Courtesy FableVision; **30** br imagebroker/Alamy; **30** tl (c) Kevin Schafer/CORBIS; **30** bkgd tl age fotostock/SuperStock; **30-31** bkgd age fotostock/SuperStock; **32-33** bkgd Edward Parker/Alamy; **31** br MICHAEL & PATRICIA FOGDEN/Minden Pictures; **31** tr (c) Kevin Schafer/CORBIS; **32** tr Michael & Patricia Fogden/Getty Images; **33** tr (c) Kevin Schafer/Corbis; **33** bkgd tr age fotostock/SuperStock; **37** br Rubberball/Jupiter Images; **38** cl (c) Tom Bean/CORBIS; **38** cr (c) Louie Psihoyos/CORBIS; **38** bl David McNew/Getty Images; **38** br (c) Louie Psihoyos/CORBIS; **38** t (c) Jonathan Blair/Corbis; **39** tl Louie Psihoyos/Getty Images; **39** tc Mark Wilson/Newsmakers; **39** tr (c) Richard T. Nowitz/CORBIS; **39** bl MICHAEL ANDREWS/Animals Animals - Earth Scenes; **39** bc blickwinkel/Alamy; **39** br (c) Garry Adams/Index Stock Imagery; **40-41** b Christian Jegou/Photo Researchers, Inc.; **42** Courtesy T.V. Padma;